LEARN TO

Read Music

EQUIVALENT TERMS
(US AND EUROPEAN)

Musical terms vary from country to country. Here are some of the most commonly used terms and their equivalents.

US	EUROPEAN
Note length	
Whole note	Semibreve
Half note	Minim
Quarter note	Crotchet
Eighth note	Quaver
Sixteenth note	Semiquaver
Thirty-second note	Demi-semiquaver
Tempo	
Slow, stately	Largo
Slow	Adagio
Walking pace	Andante
Quick, lively	Allegro
Fairly quick	Allegretto
Lively, quick	Vivace
Dynamics	
Loud	Forte
Very loud	Fortissimo
Soft	Piano
Very soft	Pianissimo
Getting louder	Crescendo
Getting softer	Decrescendo

© 2005 by Carlton Books Ltd.

This 2005 edition published by Metro Books, by arrangement with Carlton Books Ltd.

Music Consultant: Andrew O'Brien
Design Manager: Michelle Pickering
Edited by: Mike Flynn
Production: Lisa French
CD recorded at the Piano Factory, London and produced by The Orgone Company

Metro Books
122 Fifth Avenue
New York, NY 10011

ISBN–13: 978-0-7607-7054-2
ISBN–10: 0-7607-7054-9

Printed and bound in Dubai

10 9 8 7 6

LEARN TO

Read Music

TERENCE ASHLEY

METRO BOOKS

NEW YORK

Contents

FOREWORD

Hello There...

Music is a language and like any language it has rules and structures that can be learned by anyone who cares to take the time to do so. At times you might feel that you are facing an uphill struggle, but with a little perseverance and an awful lot of practice you will soon be reading music, if not fluently then at least with a degree of confidence that will allow you to develop into a much better player.

IT WON'T HURT A BIT

In an ideal world, we would all learn to read music while learning to play our instruments. Unfortunately, we don't live in an ideal world and so very many of us are forced to play catch-up. This is particularly the case with those instruments, such as the electric guitar, which lie at the rock 'n' roll end of the music spectrum. All too often, players will develop great technical ability without ever feeling the need to read a note of music. This is a shame, because by doing so they are cutting themselves off from the truly vast catalogue of music that is available.

Learn to Read Music is an audio-visual tutor. Over the course of 10 lessons, you will develop a basic understanding of sight-reading while being given a firm grounding in the general principles of music theory. New ideas are introduced in stages, which become more complex as you progress through this tutor. Frequent exercises designed to test your understanding of the material can be found throughout the book and by the time you complete this course you should be able to handle just about any piece of music that might be put in front of you.

This tutor holds something for everyone, from the beginner who would like to start by building a firm. foundation to the expert player who until now has remained musically illiterate. You'll find that some things in music are universal, so that the lesson learned

LISTENING AND READING

Throughout this tutor each lesson is backed up with a series of sound and sight tests. You'll know when they are coming because you'll see a shaded box containing an "ear" symbol. Whenever you see this sign you will be asked questions based on tracks on the CD.

A box containing an "eye" symbol warns of a coming performance or reading test. You will be asked to identify aspects of musical notation, or perhaps to sing or play the example on your instrument. You can check the accuracy of your answers by listening to the CD that comes with this tutor.

USING THE TUTOR CD

Learn to Read Music comes with a 55-minute compact disc. This has two purposes. The first is to provide aural back-up for any new concepts. For example, if the notation presents you with a long series of notes you will be able to hear exactly what they sound like, which should help you to appreciate the link between the notation and the music. Pattern recognition, be it of note or rhythm patterns, is key to developing the skill of sight-reading. Secondly, the compact disc is loaded with exercise material that will enable you to test your own understanding of each lesson. An instruction to play the CD is shown by the "PLAY" symbol.

In addition to the "PLAY," you will also find two numbers indicating track and index points, which you will need to programme into your CD player.

☞ 🎵 1/3

The first number is ALWAYS the same as the number of the lesson. The index numbers, which work on most CD players, are like tracks within tracks. These can usually be programmed in the same way. The example shown above instructs you to listen to the first exercise in lesson 3. Don't worry too much if your CD player doesn't show index points, as these tracks play through sequentially and can just as easily be controlled via the pause button. If you have a remote control unit this will be a simple operation.

here can be applied to any style, be it jazz, rock, classical or the blues. And don't feel you have to play an instrument to benefit from this tutor: singers should have no trouble following these exercises.

THE BEST APPROACH

One of the joys of working on your own rather than in a group or class setting is that you can work entirely at your own speed. There should be nothing in this tutor that would give you any real trouble and if anything you may find yourself progressing faster than you imagined. Don't be fooled, however, into thinking that you will be a competent sight-reader by the end of this course. Sight-reading—which is the ability to be able to see a piece of music and play it perfectly at the first attempt—is a skill that takes a long time to develop and calls for a great deal of practice. Try, if you can, to avoid the obvious trap of using your ears to figure out where the music is going. That isn't sight-reading; that's guesswork.

In order to get the best out of this tutor you should begin by setting yourself a timetable and resolving to stick to it. While you may be able to plough through a lesson in as short a space as an hour, your time might be better spent devoting an entire week to the contents of a single lesson, thereby ensuring that you get the maximum benefit from each and every one. While doing this, you can also visit your local library and take out some published sheet music, which will give you "real world" examples from which to work. Before you begin each new lesson, make certain that you have understood the previous one fully. A brief summary can be found at the end of each lesson.

Finally, here's a guarantee of success. If you take the time and trouble to play through a little music every day, perhaps just for five minutes at a time, then within a year or so you will be able to handle just about any kind of notation, no matter how demanding. Now get reading!

TERENCE ASHLEY
LONDON, OCTOBER 2004

INTRODUCTION

Time to get Historical

Music has certainly been around almost as long as we have. For most of this time it has been passed from generation to generation by means of song, in much the same way as the oral tradition has seen myths and legends come down to us through story telling. It has only been during the last thousand years or so, however, that we have been equipped with the means to write music down.

THE CLASSICAL WORLD

Before music was written down, the musician of old was faced with limited choices. He or she could either attempt to play something that they already knew or they could wing it and try making something up on the spot. This could make for some wonderful music, but there was also the danger that it might just be awful. With the development of formal notation the chance element was removed; some musicians consider this to be a failing of written notation. What was gained, however, was continuity. For the first time, musicians could build on the advances of the previous generations and leave a legacy for those who followed. Best of all, it allowed the work of the truly talented composers to be retained and preserved, and indeed it is with the development of formal notation that one sees the true greats—Bach, Mozart, Beethoven—begin to emerge and have a very real influence on the development of music in the West.

It would be interesting at this point to compare the development of composition (and notation) in the West with the classical traditions of other cultures. When we think of music by Bach, Mozart or Beethoven we tend to imagine works of genius that have been all but carved into stone, preserved intact for succeeding generations. To a certain extent this is certainly true, but why shouldn't it be this way? Just imagine what might have happened had the music been diluted by reinterpretation by lesser talents as the music was passed down through the generations and diluted by lesser talents with each step. Even worse might be the attempt to pass on complex orchestral arrangements by any means other than clear, standard notation.

OTHER CULTURES

Interestingly, the music of other cultures does not necessarily lend itself to accurate interpretation via our standard notation. It is a sad fact that the Western tonal system may be inadequate to deal with musical forms that are often completely alien to Western ears. We divide the octave into 12 equal divisions (the notes A to G on a piano keyboard if you include the black notes), but other cultures, especially those of India and China, have many more, and more subtle, divisions to deal with.

We are all familiar with the song "Do-Re-Mi" from *The Sound of Music*. It is built on the European "Sol-fa" system, which gives singable names to the notes of the scale, producing the pattern "Do," "Re," "Mi," "Fa," "So," "La," "Ti," and "Do." This approach has the benefit of making it easier to teach melodies to those who can't read music. Other musical cultures also have a version of this, known as solmization, which assigns names to each degree of a scale using a phonetic syllable. Examples from other cultures include the Indian "Sa," "Ri," "Ga," "Ma," "Pa," "Dha," "Ni," the Chinese "Kung," "Shang," "Chiao," "Chih," "Yü," and "Ding," "Dong," "Deng," "Dung," "Dang" from Bali.

DOTS ON A PAGE

Anyone looking at a piece of Western notation would recognize it immediately, even if they didn't have a clue what any of it was trying to convey. We know that those dots are notes, and some people may even notice that a few of the dots exist only in one line. The fact that they are arranged on a five-line stave might suggest something about the pitch of the notes, and the way they are grouped is suggestive, perhaps, of a rhythmic pattern. Further use of symbols and other graphics give clues as to the tempo and style of performance. In short, we have all of the information we need to turn the dots on the page into music in our ears, a process that has taken a mere thousand years or so.

THE ORAL TRADITION LIVES ON

A late arrival to the music scene, which despite its modernity has its roots very firmly in the oral tradition, has thrown up a potential rival to musical notation as a means of preserving the integrity of the composer's work. The development of music technology means that we can now listen repeatedly to a performance of a piece of music, a performance that may in fact be by the original composer. At a stroke this removes any arguments about the composer's intentions and may yet prove to be a series rival to notated music.

THE EVOLUTION OF MUSICAL NOTATION

There is evidence, albeit scant, to suggest that the Ancient Egyptians used some form of notation to record their musical ideas some five thousand years ago. But Western musical notation as we understand it might truly be said to have begun its evolution in the seat of civilization, Ancient Greece. It was the Greeks who first adopted the practice of giving names to different pitches, assigning a letter to each. Despite this, and even with a few remaining fragments of the originals, we sadly have no way of knowing how this music would have sounded. We can be certain, however, that the great philosophers of Ancient Greece had an enormous influence on the development of our system of musical theory.

The most influential of the early theoreticians were the Pythagoreans, who quite naturally saw a link between music and mathematics. Pythagoras, who lived around 550 BC, was said to have calculated the way in which pitch changed when the length of a vibrating string was altered. His followers built on his observations and even drew up a list of the mathematical ratios that were needed to create the most pleasing intervals. Halving the length of the string, they discovered, created the octave—the same note, but in a higher register. Similarly, they found that ratios of 4:3 and 3:2 produced the most pleasing intervals (known to the modern musician as the "perfect 4th" and "perfect 5th" respectively). In effect, the Pythagoreans defined what we think of as consonant sound (as opposed to dissonant sound).

Within two hundred years of Pythagoras, the influence of Plato and Aristotle could also be seen on the most important of the Ancient Greek music theorists, Aristoxenus. A former pupil of Aristotle, Aristoxenus wrote the earliest known treatise on musical theory. He was the first theoretician to put forward the view that pitch was a long line within which an infinite number of subdivisions could exist. This eventually led to the naming of specific pitches, with letters taken from the Ionian alphabet. Under the influence of the church, some of the terminology used at this time would re-emerge in Europe almost a thousand years later.

CHURCH MUSIC

Considering the influence of the church in Europe during the last thousand or so years, it should come as no surprise to find that this institution had a significant, indeed primary, influence on the development of Western notation. This began in the ninth century with the development of Christian plainchant, which we now know as NEUMIC NOTATION. Initially, this was little more than a set of instructions for singers who were already familiar with the melody, with "simple neumes" used to represent pitch directions (up or down) and vocal ornamentation. By around the year 1100, the system had developed, with the neumes laid out so as to suggest melody lines. Pitches were fixed by marking the neumes on four horizontal lines of music, representing the pitch of the note. For the first time, this enabled a singer to perform an unfamiliar melody.

For a while colors were used to give lines of music a context. For example, one line would be drawn in red to signify the note C (thus defining the notes on the other staves). Eventually, the letter of the key note was positioned at the start of the staff. The notes F, G, and C were used for this purpose and were gradually stylized, evolving into the clef symbols that are still found in music today.

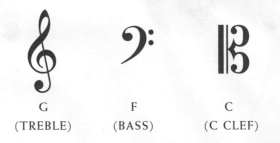

G
(TREBLE)

F
(BASS)

C
(C CLEF)

ARISTOXENUS AND FRANCO

Neumic notation began gradually to take on some of the characteristics of the modern system, including the addition of the fifth staff line. Time values were first applied to notes in around 1260 when a system we now know as MENSURAL NOTATION was codified by Franco of Cologne. Under the influence of Aristoxenus, he devised a system of notes made up of proportional subdivisions. The note values were known by the names *maxima*, *long*, *breve*, *semibreve*, and *minim*—the latter three terms remain in use today. Rather than the elliptical-shaped dots that we use today, these appeared on the staff as filled squares or diamond-shapes with stems.

Franco also made it possible to split the named notes into subdivisions of either two or three to accommodate a variety of different rhythmic effects. By combining these different note values it became possible to produce a wider variety of rhythmic effects.

Further subdivisions had been added by around 1400 to allow the notation of music of greater subtlety These subdivisions—the *fusa* (sometimes called the semi-minim) and the *semifusa*—were indicated with one or two "flags" on top of the stems.

MODAL MUSIC AND THE MODERN SYSTEM

From around 1600 the mensural system gradually evolved into the earliest form of the notation we now recognize. It was during this period that the notes took on their familiar elliptical shape and began to be grouped together according to their values. The system of perfect and imperfect notes was abandoned and from this point onwards the modern system of time values adopted. It was during this phase that the dotted note first appeared. (We'll be looking at dotted notes later in the tutor.)

It was also during this period that music acquired a new harmonic structure. Until this point, music written for plainsong, such as Gregorian chanting, had invariably been composed using notes that had been drawn from a series of sequences known as MODES. The modes were scales made up from a fixed set of pitch intervals, each with its own unique character. So distinctive are these modes that, during the Middle Ages, melodies were listed according to their mode in liturgical books or tonaries. The eight modes used were Dorian, Hypodorian, Phrygian, Hypophrygian, Lydian, Hypolydian, Mixolydian, and Hypomixolydian.

The Renaissance saw the creation of four new modes, of which the most important were the Aeolian and Ionian. During the seventeenth century these two new modes came into widespread use, evolving into the major and minor scale systems that have come to dominate Western music. The basic difference between the modal system and the scale system was that while the modes were made up of fixed notes, the major and minor systems took the intervals of steps and half-steps from the Aeolian and Ionian modes and applied them across the entire range of notes.

NOTATION NOW

Since the introduction of the major and minor scale systems the principle additions to the Western style of musical notation has been the extensive use of shorthand terms to denote changes in the way music should be played. These can indicate anything from changes in tempo to instruction on the dynamics of the piece of music.

Unfortunately, traditional music notation has sometimes proved inflexible, driving some contemporary composers to develop entirely new approaches. However, the traditional system continues to evolve and remains almost universally accepted.

TABLATURE

Tablature is a system of musical notation that dates back almost as far as the more conventional notes on a staff. It is used to give more detailed instructions to players of fretted stringed instruments, such as the guitar and the lute, and is still commonly used by guitarists today. Tablature is a schematic representation of the instrument's fingerboard. Six horizontal lines represent the strings; numbers positioned on these lines indicate where the notes are fretted.

The example shown below represents tablature at its simplest. Regular notation above the tablature provides clues to rhythmic structure of the piece. Tablature can also be written using standard ornamentation, which provides the player with rhythmic and dynamic instructions.

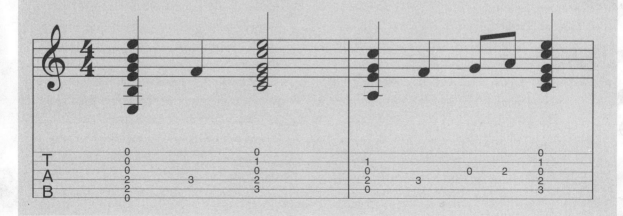

 Pitch

Try singing the opening notes of a song that everyone will know, such as "When The Saints Go Marching In." As you sing the opening line—"Oh, when the saints..."— you will notice that it's made up of four notes, and that each of these is completely different from the other and that the sound of the notes rises as you progress. This variation between the notes is called PITCH.

HIGH AND LOW NOTES

If you play "When The Saints Go Marching In" on the piano you will find that each successive note would be to the right of the previous one. Playing a note to the right of the one you have just played makes the pitch HIGHER; moving in the opposite direction makes it LOWER. On a stringed instrument, moving the hand along the fingerboard towards the bridge raises the pitch; moving towards the tuning pegs lowers the pitch.

Every note you hear has its own pitch. This is obvious when looking at a piano. A pitch is a fixed sound that can be identified using a series of letters ranging from A to G. 🖝 💿 1/1

OH   WHEN THE SAINTS...

TWELVE HALF STEPS

By doubling the frequency of a note one can increase its pitch by an octave. In the West the octave is divided into 12 equal divisions, known as HALF STEPS. Playing through each of these divisions will cause you to move from the starting note to the octave in 12 steps. This can best be illustrated on a piano keyboard. Listen to track 1/2 of the CD and you will hear the complete range of notes within a single octave starting from the note of A. 🖝 💿 1/2

HEARING OCTAVES

Here is an experiment for you to try out. Start to hum a note, holding the pitch steady for a few seconds. Now gradually increase the pitch while you are humming. At one point—and you'll know immediately when this happens— you will hit a note which naturally sounds very similar to the one you started with. Even though this new note is clearly higher in pitch than the original, both of them would be given the same name. These two notes which you have just sung are separated in pitch by a fixed interval called an "octave."

Our first exercise is a simple test of your ability to recognize pitch changes. Over the next eight tracks on the CD, you will hear eight sets of four-note sequences. Three of the notes in each set will have the same pitch, but one will be different. Your task is to identify the odd one out in each group—A, B, C or D (answers on page 120).

1. ☞ 🎵 1/3   2. ☞ 🎵 1/4

3. ☞ 🎵 1/5   4. ☞ 🎵 1/6

5. ☞ 🎵 1/7   6. ☞ 🎵 1/8

7. ☞ 🎵 1/9   8. ☞ 🎵 1/10

THE NAMES OF THE NOTES

A range of letters running from A and G is used to name all of the white notes on a piano keyboard (we'll get to the black notes a little later). These same seven notes are represented in standard notation using a grid of five horizontal lines known as a STAFF or STAVE (but always STAVES in the plural). A variety of elliptically shaped symbols are placed on or between the lines to indicate the pitch of a note and how long it lasts.

Unfortunately, as you can see below, this only allows for a range of nine different pitches—clearly there are a good many more than that. We get around this problem by positioning what is known as a CLEF symbol at the front of the staff. (There are a number of different types of clef, although the most common is the treble clef.) It is also known as a G CLEF, because the center of the figure always starts on the second line from the bottom. This defines that line as representing the note G. This, in turn, means that we can work out all the other notes on the treble clef from that point.

The diagram below shows how the treble clef is used to represent notes on a keyboard. ☞ 🎵 1/11

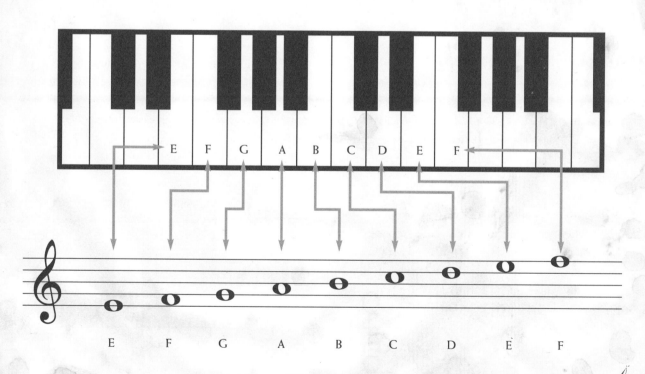

LEDGER LINES

An obvious limitation of the staff as it appears on the previous page is that it can only be used to represent a narrow range of pitches—from E on the bottom line to F on the top line. This range can, however, be extended through the use of what are known as "ledger lines." Quite simply, where a note goes off the edge of the staff, additional short lines can be added for that note only. A range of more than two octaves can be achieved using this method, which is shown below.

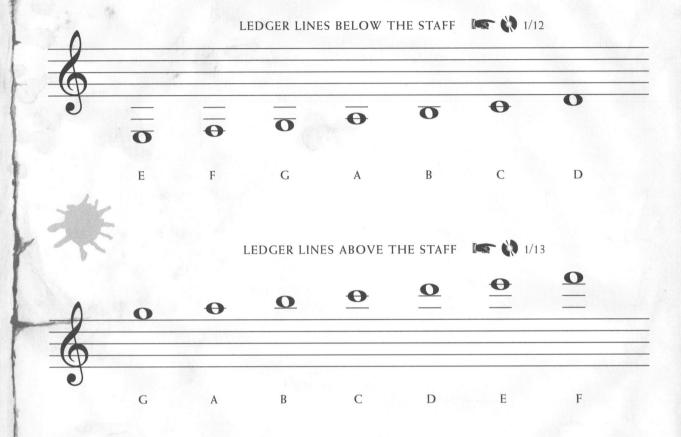

LEDGER LINES BELOW THE STAFF 1/12

E F G A B C D

LEDGER LINES ABOVE THE STAFF 1/13

G A B C D E F

MNEMONIC PHRASES

The lines and spaces that make up the staff are always named from the bottom upwards. This means that the bottom line is always known as the first line and the top line the fifth line. The space between lines are treated in the same way. There are five lines and four spaces in total.

Learning to name the lines and spaces is a fundamental part of sight-reading. There have been many different approaches to getting novices to the point where they can identify a note automatically. Most of these rely on the use of mnemonic phrases as memory aids. The notes on the line of treble staff are E-G-B-D-F. These can be learned by remembering the phrase "EVERY GOOD BOY DESERVES FAVORS," or sometimes "EAT GOOD BREAD DEAR FATHER."

You'll will find that just about every music teacher has his or her own preferred method of jogging the memory. Because they spell out the word "FACE" the notes in the spaces are much easier to remember.

TEST 2

Each of the following five staves of music has eight differently pitched notes. Your task is simply to name each note shown below. This might seem like a simple enough task were it not for the fact that some of the notes occur on ledger lines and so will have to be worked out at this stage. This might be the time to try out the mnemonic phrases that we mentioned earlier. On a treble staff they are "EAT GOOD BREAD DEAR FATHER" for notes on the lines, and "FACE" for those on the spaces. You can check your answers on page 120 when you've completed the test.

EXERCISE 1.

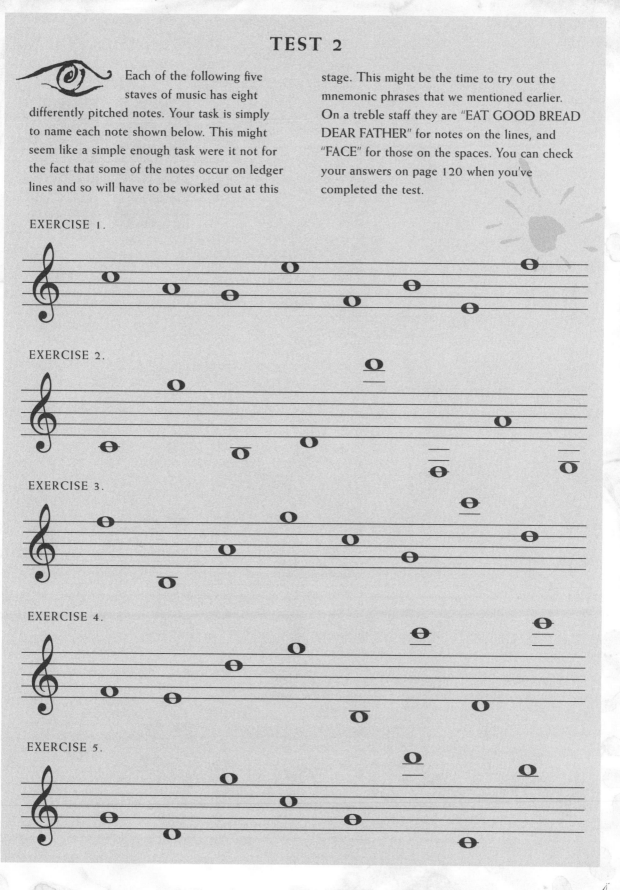

EXERCISE 2.

EXERCISE 3.

EXERCISE 4.

EXERCISE 5.

THE BASS CLEF

We have, so far, looked at a range of notes covering just over three octaves—E on the lowest ledger line to G on the highest ledger line. That's a range of just 39 notes (if you include the black notes); a standard modern grand piano has a range of over seven octaves. The extra notes are displayed in written music by using a different kind of clef—the BASS CLEF.

Substituting a bass clef for the treble clef means that the lines and spaces of that staff take on different names and pitches. The lines of the bass clef can be remembered using the phrase "GOOD BOYS DESERVE FUN ALWAYS," and the spaces with "All COWS EAT GRASS."

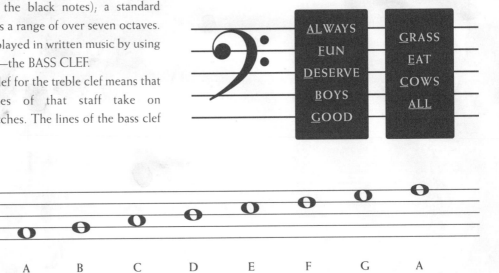

1/14

| G | A | B | C | D | E | F | G | A |

ADDING LEDGER LINES

We can extend the range of notes on a bass staff by adding ledger lines. In this case, they move from F downward and from B upwards. In the examples shown for both clefs only three ledger lines have been named above and below the staff. In fact, ledger lines can be notated to create far wider ranges than this. In practice, however, the music is often easier to read if these notes are shown on a staff in a different range, by using an alternative clef.

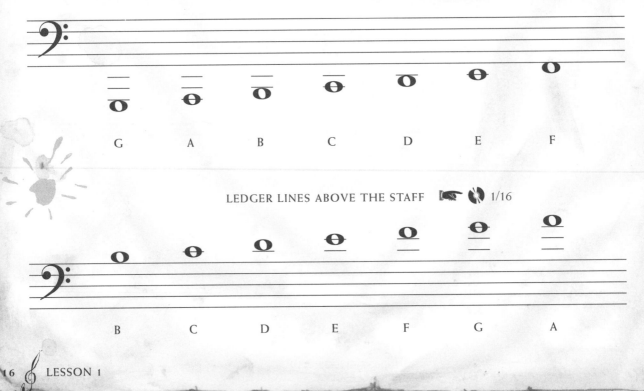

LEDGER LINES BELOW THE STAFF 1/15

| G | A | B | C | D | E | F |

LEDGER LINES ABOVE THE STAFF 1/16

| B | C | D | E | F | G | A |

TEST 3

 This exercise is really just a shortened version of the previous one, this time on the bass staff. This means that the note names are not the same as those shown on the treble staff. As before, your task is to name each note. Don't forget your mnemonic phrases: "Good Boys Deserve Fun Always" on the lines; "All Cows Eat Grass" for the spaces. You can check your answers on page 120 when you have finished the exercise.

EXERCISE 1.

EXERCISE 2.

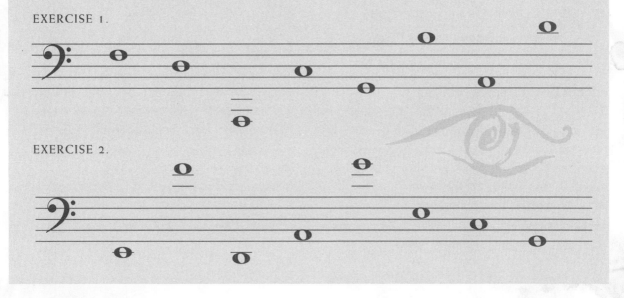

THE WHOLE RANGE

The piano has a wider range of notes than most other musical instruments, which means that music composed specifically for the piano is nearly always written over two staves that are shown concurrently. (A curly bracket indicates that the two staves are to be played simultaneously.) Although it is by no means always the case, as a general rule the pianist's left hand plays the notes on the bass staff, and the right hand plays the notes on the treble staff.

This example shows a range of nine notes played over both staves. (If you look closely you will notice that there is a crossover point where the notes could be written on either staff.) The note C in this register is referred to as MIDDLE C.   1/17

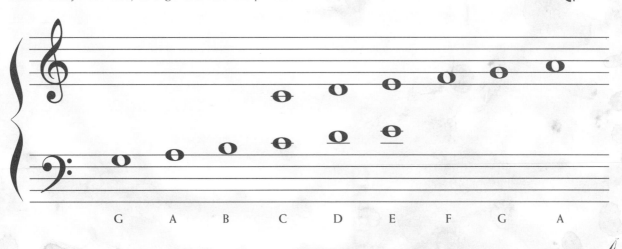

G A B C D E F G A

THE BLACK NOTES

Having concentrated our attention on naming the white notes of the piano keyboard, it's now time to turn our attention to the black notes.

The white notes have already been allocated the sequence of letters between A and G. This being the case, it seems reasonable that the black notes should take their names from the white notes they sit between. Depending on whether the black note is higher or lower in pitch than the white note it will be given the suffix of either SHARP or FLAT respectively. This is shown in music notation using the symbols "#" for a sharp and "♭" for a flat.

ENHARMONIC NOTES

If you examine the notes at the foot of the page you will see that the notes on display take their names from the surrounding white notes. This means that each of the black notes can have one of two names. It can either be named as a "sharpened" equivalent to the note immediately to its left—for example F# (referred to as "F sharp")—or else as a "flattened" version of the note immediately to its right—for example B♭ (referred to as "B flat"). Notes such as these are said to be ENHARMONIC. Although it may seem logical to do so, these names are not interchangeable. Complete accuracy in musical notation depends entirely on context. For the time being, however, you needn't worry about this as it will become clearer as you progress and get a better grasp of the rules of notation.

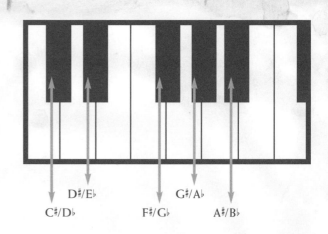

C#/D♭   D#/E♭   F#/G♭   G#/A♭   A#/B♭

WHAT ABOUT WHITE NOTES?

One could be forgiven for imagining that the names given to the white notes in the range A to G were fixed and unchangeable, but this is not always the case. There are, in fact, some situations in which it is possible for various of the white notes to take on enharmonic characteristics.

You may, in exceptional circumstances, come across the note names B#, C♭, and E#, all of which, should you check on a piano keyboard, would seem NOT to exist. Although occurring in a technical or theoretical sense, sometimes it may be necessary to follow a set of harmonic rules that require you to sharpen or flatten certain notes. If, for example, you flatten the note C—that is, you reduce its pitch by a half step—it becomes C♭, even though the pitch is identical to the note B. Similarly, and even though they are identical in pitch to the notes C and F respectively, the notes B# and E# are also valid possible names.

ENHARMONIC RULES

When indicated on the staff, flat or sharp symbols have the effect of raising or lowering, by one half step, the note that follows. All subsequent notes on the same line or space within a grouping of notes separated by vertical "barlines" remain as sharps or flats, but do not require the continued use of the symbols. A "Natural" symbol (♮) is used to indicate that the note is to revert to its original pitch within the bar.

C#   C#   C   C#   C   C#   C   C#

ENHARMONIC EQUIVALENTS

All eight enharmonic possibilities are shown alongside their alternative note names in the list below. (All notes shown below are in the treble clef.) In each case you will notice that no two enharmonic equivalents occupy the same line or space on the staff. Once you have acquired a greater understanding of the way in which scales, intervals, and chords work, then the theory behind which of the two note names is appropriate to use will become clearer. This issue will be covered in lesson 3.

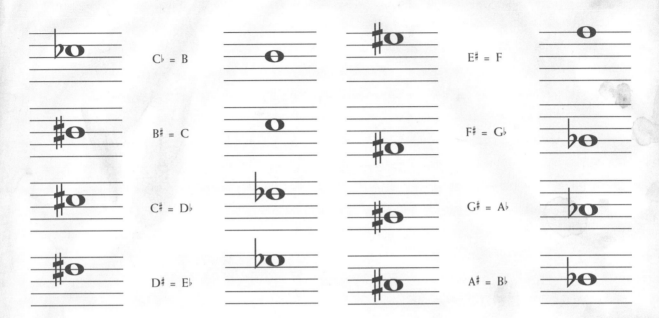

C♭ = B

B♯ = C

C♯ = D♭

D♯ = E♭

E♯ = F

F♯ = G♭

G♯ = A♭

A♯ = B♭

STEP AND HALF-STEP INTERVALS

The two staves below show the enharmonic notes laid out on two staves. The top staff treats all the enharmonic notes as sharps and the bottom staff treats them as flats. In each case the pitch of the notes (and indeed the entire sequence) will have an identical sound.

Each of the notes is separated by a half step in pitch. Although some twentieth-century composers have experimented with smaller divisions, known as microtones, in most Western music this is the smallest pitch interval. An interval of two half steps—for example, between the notes F and G—is referred to as a STEP.

Listen to the two sequences on track 1/18 of the CD. The first plays the 13 half-step intervals between C and C within an octave. The second plays just the eight white notes and is made up of intervals of steps and half steps.

 1/18

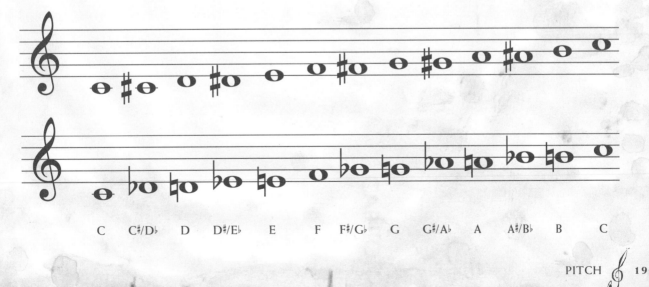

| C | C♯/D♭ | D | D♯/E♭ | E | F | F♯/G♭ | G | G♯/A♭ | A | A♯/B♭ | B | C |

TEST 4

 If you look at the five staves of music shown below you will see that each one contains eight differently pitched notes, most of which are shown either as a sharp or flat, and your task is to identify the correct note names. Pay special attention to the "NATURAL" symbols—it's quite easy to get them mixed up with the sharp signs—and don't forget that the effect of the natural symbol is to return the "SHARPENED" or "FLATTENED" note to its original pitch—a half step higher or lower. Turn to page 120 for the answers.

TEST 5

Before you decide on your answers to this very demanding listening test, you should review it several times.(Each of the staves below has an equivalent track on the CD.) In each case, one of the four notes is wrong—but the other three are correct. Your task is to identify which is the odd note. Begin each exercise by working out the note names and then singing or playing them for yourself until you are familiar with the pattern or tune. You should then listen to the relevant track on the CD. If you are singing the exercises and don't have a pitch reference, you can use the first note of the sequence to get your bearings. As ever, when you are ready you can check your answers on page 120.

EXERCISE 1. 1/19

EXERCISE 2. 1/20

EXERCISE 3. 1/21

EXERCISE 4. 1/22

EXERCISE 5. 1/23

EXERCISE 6. 1/24

TIME OUT: SUMMARY OF LESSON 1

Below is a summary of the key points of this lesson. If you find yourself in any doubt about anything in the list you should review it before moving on to the next lesson.

- Meaning of pitch
- Meaning of octave
- Understanding of the staff
- Understanding of ledger lines
- Naming the notes on a treble clef
- Naming the notes on the bass clef
- Understanding flats and sharps
- Understanding enharmonic equivalents
- Understanding the "natural" symbol
- Difference between steps and half steps

Timing and Rhythm

Although it may take a while to become second nature, you should by now be able at least to identify the names of notes written on the staff. But while the note name tells you the pitch of the note that is to be played or sung, it fails to indicate when the note should be played, or how long it should be sustained. In this lesson we will be examining note values.

FEELING THE RHYTHM

Music, like a living body, has a distinct pulse. This is the RHYTHM of music. As you tap your foot along to the music you will almost certainly find yourself drawn to a consistent beat. Irrespective of the TEMPO of the music—i.e. how fast it is being played—the time interval between each tap will be the same value as all of the others.

By far the most common type of beat you will hear groups together four QUARTER NOTES. You will often find that that you can count along to most types of music by repeating the numbers one to four. In doing so, you will usually find that music naturally emphasizes the first beat, or the "ONE." This natural grouping of beats is known as a BAR.

Obviously, the same principle applies to the time values of notes sung or played using an instrument. A QUARTER NOTE is shown in written music as a filled ellipse with a "stem." The stem can point in either direction, depending on the position of the note on the staff. Usually, notes that are on and above the

third line have downwards-pointing stems, while below that the notes have upwards-pointing stems.

QUARTER NOTE

At the foot of the page is a piece of music made up of two bars. The two numbers piled up next to the treble clef at the beginning of the staff make up what is known as the TIME SIGNATURE.

The number four written above another four denotes that the piece is in FOUR-FOUR time, and that there are four beats in the bar. The FOUR-FOUR time signature is so commonly used for just about every style of music that it has come to be known as COMMON TIME. If you listen to track 2/1 of the CD you will hear the notes being played to an accompanying rhythmic click.

2/1

THE VALUES OF NOTES

So far, all of the notes we have dealt with have been of the same duration, or value. Yet singing even the simplest tune reveals that some notes are likely to last longer than others. Mathematician and philosopher Gottfried Wilhelm von Leibniz (1646–1716) once described music as "unconscious arithmetic." So it should come as no surprise to find that mathematics plays a part in determining the duration of notes, with a notation that follows strict mathematical principles.

FILLING THE BAR

Note values are fixed properties that are measured against the WHOLE NOTE. The note value which forms the beat in the vast majority of Western music is the quarter note. The whole note can be subdivided four times by the quarter note. It is helpful to think of all note values as multiples or divisions of the quarter note. Most of the subdivisions that follow are written against a time signature of four-four, which means that each beat in the bar last for the equivalent of a quarter note.

WHOLE NOTES

The WHOLE NOTE, which sustains over four beats, is the longest note value we usually find in Western music. The note is sustained for the amount of time it takes to count the four beats of the bar. The whole note has no stem and is shown on the staff as a hollow ellipse.

WHOLE NOTE

The upper staff at the bottom of the page is made up of a single whole note. If you listen to track 2/2 on the CD you will hear how the note sustains over four beats, which are audible as clicks. You can count along with the beats, numbered one to four, throughout the four bars of this example.

HALF NOTE

The HALF NOTE is sustained for two beats of a bar of music that is in four-four time. This half note appears in written notation as a hollow circle, just like the whole note, but with an added stem.

HALF NOTE

If you listen to track 2/3 of the CD you will hear the two half notes that appear in the staff at the bottom of the page. Four bars of this example can be heard on the CD.

WHOLE-NOTE BAR (FOUR BEATS) 2/2

ONE   TWO   THREE   FOUR

HALF-NOTE BAR (TWO BEATS) 2/3

ONE   TWO   THREE   FOUR

FURTHER DIVISIONS

The QUARTER NOTE can be subdivided into EIGHTH NOTES, SIXTEENTH NOTES, THIRTY-SECOND NOTES, and even SIXTY-FOURTH NOTES. Once again, the descriptions that follow all assume that a basic time signature of four-four is being used, thus each beat has the value of a quarter note.

EIGHTH NOTE

An EIGHTH NOTE has half the timing value of a quarter note. In a bar with a time signature of four-four an eighth note will sustain for half a beat. It appears on the staff as a quarter note with a curly line drawn from the end of the stem. This is known as a FLAG or a TAIL.

EIGHTH NOTE

Groups of two or four eighth notes can be joined together with a BEAM, which makes the notes easier to read

A beam is a line that joins the tips of two or more stems and is applied in whichever direction the stem is pointing.

SIXTEENTH NOTES

A note which is a quarter of the value of a quarter note is called a SIXTEENTH NOTE. It can be identified from the double flag on its stem.

SIXTEENTH NOTE

Sixteenth notes can also be grouped together by a beam. A sixteenth-note beam consists of two horizontal lines that join the tip of the stem.

OTHER DIVISIONS

A sixteenth note can be halved again to produce a thirty-second note—an eighth of a quarter note. A further subdivision to a sixteenth of a quarter note is also possible—this is known as a sixty-fourth note—but this is rare.

THIRTY-SECOND NOTE   SIXTY-FOURTH NOTE

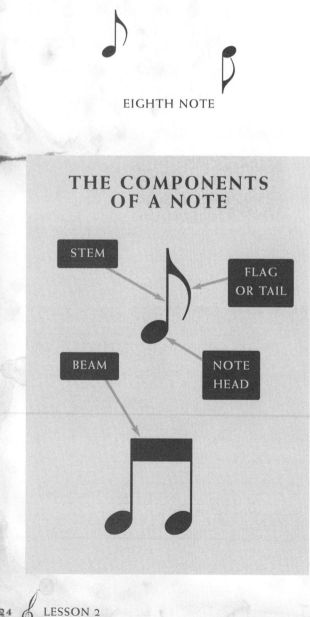

THE COMPONENTS OF A NOTE

STEM

FLAG OR TAIL

BEAM

NOTE HEAD

HOW TO COUNT NOTES

The four staves shown below each contain a single bar of notes. The first contains four quarter notes, each of which has a duration of a single beat. By now you should be familiar with counting in fours, so this is just for reference.

Example two contains eight eighth notes—or half beats. It's quite common to count eighth notes by inserting the word "and" between each of the beats. If you take a listen to tracks 2/4 and 2/5 on the CD, you will hear that the tempo of the beats on the two staves is identical. In the latter example, however, there are four additional note sounds inserted in the spaces between each beat. These notes should be "felt" rather than counted.

SIXTEENTH NOTES AND BEYOND

It is very difficult to count divisions of sixteenth notes and beyond. At a slow tempo it is possible to split the syllables, so that you count out ONE-UN-AN-AND-TWO-OO-AN-AND-THREE-EE-AN-AND-FOUR-OR-AN-AND. At a faster tempo, or where thirty-second notes are involved, you will not be able to count that quickly. As an alternative, some people like to multiply the numbering, splitting a bar of four-four into a count of eight or even sixteen.

QUARTER-NOTE BAR (ONE BEAT) 2/4

ONE   TWO   THREE   FOUR

EIGHT-NOTE BAR (HALF BEATS) 2/5

ONE   AND   TWO   AND   THREE   AND   FOUR   AND

SIXTEENTH-NOTE BAR (QUARTER BEATS) 2/6

ONE   AND   TWO   AND   THREE   AND   FOUR   AND

THIRTY-SECOND NOTE BAR (EIGHTH BEATS) 2/7

ONE   AND   TWO   AND   THREE   AND   FOUR   AND

COMBINING NOTE VALUES

So far we have seen how notes are grouped, for convenience, into bars according to the the time signature of the piece of music, which is indicated by the numbers at the beginning of the staff. All of the music we have seen so far has been in four-four time. This means that the value of the notes in a bar add up to four quarter beats. This is also the case for a bar of eight eighth notes, sixteen sixteenth notes, and so on. Music, of whatever type, takes its natural rhythm from the way the notes of the piece are grouped or accented within the bar. Rhythmic effects are created by the combinations of patterns within bars and it is rare to find bars of music where different time values have not been combined in this way.

In the following example, look at the two staves shown below. Count out the note values on each beat as shown beneath each note. Remember that a quarter note lasts for one beat, a half note for two beats, and a whole note for four beats. Now tap or clap out the rhythm according to the note values. This means tapping ONLY on the first beat of the note. Thus the sequence will be TAP-TAP-TAP-SILENCE-TAP-TAP-TAP-SILENCE-TAP-TAP-TAP-TAP-TAP-SILENCE-SILENCE-SILENCE. (In reality, of course, each beat of silence represents the previous note being sustained—this exercise is designed to illustrate how the rhythm is created.) Try now to put the two together, tapping out the rhythm and counting out the beat values at the same time.

The combined time value of the bar is always four. The first two bars each contain two quarter notes and a half note (1+1+2 beats = 4 beats). The third bar has four quarter notes (1+1+1+1 beats = 4 beats). The fourth bar contains one whole note (4 beats = 4 beats). 2/8

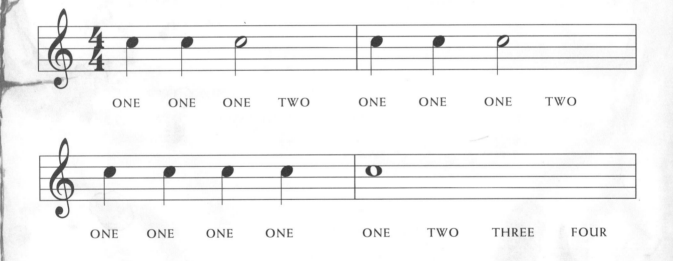

ONE ONE ONE TWO ONE ONE ONE TWO

ONE ONE ONE ONE ONE TWO THREE FOUR

ADDING THE EIGHTH NOTES

The example shown below makes use of eighth notes. Because these are harder to count—their value is half a beat—you must count out two eighth notes for every single beat. Adopt the approach you took with the previous exercise, counting out the beats as shown below the staff and then tapping out the rhythm of the note values. 2/9

ONE ONE-AND-ONE-AND-ONE-AND ONE ONE-AND ONE TWO

TEST 6

Here are a further five two-bar exercises for you to work through which will extend the theme of understanding the way note values are used to create rhythms. In each exercise you must name the note value and be able to tap out the rhythm correctly. You should not be concerned with the pitch of the note—which is the C above middle C—only its time value. You'll notice that exercise five contains sixteenth notes. Don't forget that four sixteenth notes are equivalent to a quarter note and need to be counted out accordingly.

EXERCISE 1. 2/10

EXERCISE 2. 2/11

EXERCISE 3. 2/12

EXERCISE 4. 2/13

EXERCISE 5. 2/14

OTHER NOTE VALUES

The note values outlined on the previous six pages can be thought of as the basic units of musical currency. That said, however, it still leaves us with a relatively limited palette from which to draw. As they stand, the combinations that you can create with the palette you have so far are simply too limited to express the complexities of most forms of music. Because of this we need to look at ways of, for example, creating a note that will last for three beats. Similarly, there may well be musical phrases that require a note to be sustained across two bars. How are we going to achieve that?

DOTS AND TIES

Adding a dot to any standard note has the effect of lengthening that note by half of its value. For example, a half note followed by a dot—referred to as a DOTTED HALF NOTE—has a value of three quarter-note beats.

= 3 QUARTER-NOTE BEATS

= 1½ QUARTER-NOTE BEATS

= ¾ OF A QUARTER-NOTE BEAT

The same effect can also be achieved by using a curved line known as a TIE. The tie is often used to link notes of different values, creating one note whose value is that of the two notes combined. For example, a half note tied to a quarter note has a value of three quarter-note beats (2 + 1 beats = 3 beats).

= 3 QUARTER-NOTE BEATS

Dots and ties are both perfectly valid ways of combining notes in order to alter their values and it is often personal choice that will determine which one a composer uses. An essential difference occurs, however, when one uses the ties to combine notes across the bar line, something that cannot be achieved with the use of a dot. In the first example shown below the final note of the first bar is tied to the half note of the second bar. This creates a three-beat count across the bar line. It should be remembered, however, that the second note in a tied pair is never, ever played.

Notes are always joined at the head. If the stem points downwards the tie is above the note; if the stem points upwards, the tie is below the note.

In the second example, you will see that there is no difference in effect between the dotted half note and the quarter note tied to the half note—both are sustained for three beats. You can hear the effect of dots and ties on the CD.  2/15

TAKING A BREAK

Strange as it may seem, possibly the most important element in music is the use of silence. Without it music would very quickly descend into noise. Musical notation has a whole set of symbols—called rests—designed to convey silence, or the absence of notes. These symbols work in exactly the same way as other musical notations except that they are instruction in what NOT to play. The most commonly used rests are shown in the panel on the right and most are straightforward in uses although you should beware of confusing the whole note and half note rests. If you look closely you'll see that the whole note rest always hangs down from the fourth line.

SPOTTING THE DIFFERENCE

A rest can sometimes be hard to spot when listening to music, especially if it is for a relatively small note value such as an eighth note. Natural expression points in the music, where the performer has added a little of their own interpretation, can sound exactly like rests.

In the example shown below you will hear what a quarter-note rest sounds like in relation to a half note. The first example features a half note at the end of the first bar followed by another at the start of the second bar. In the second version you will hear the effect of the substitution of the half notes for quarter notes combined with quarter-note rests. It is vital to remember that nothing is played when a rest is indicated. This is true for both the first and second bars of the second example. ☞ 🕭 2/16

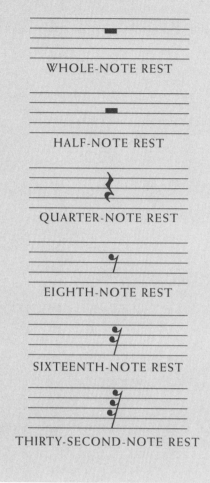

REST VALUES

Every type of note has an equivalent rest. The most common are listed below.

WHOLE-NOTE REST

HALF-NOTE REST

QUARTER-NOTE REST

EIGHTH-NOTE REST

SIXTEENTH-NOTE REST

THIRTY-SECOND-NOTE REST

ONE   ONE   ONE   TWO   ONE   TWO   ONE   AND   ONE

ONE   ONE   ONE   (TWO)   ONE   (TWO)   ONE   AND   ONE

USING OTHER RESTS

In the example below, the first bar contains a half-note rest—it lasts for two quarter-note beats. If you count out the rhythm of the piece it should sound like this: <u>ONE</u>-SILENCE-SILENCE-<u>ONE</u>.

The second bar begins with a beamed group of three eighth notes followed by an eighth-note rest and a half note. The count is <u>ONE</u>-AND-<u>TWO</u>-(SILENT "AND")-<u>ONE</u>-AND-TWO-AND.

ADDING UP

A bar made up from a half note, a quarter note, and a quarter-note rest still adds up to four beats. When you total the note values within a bar, a rest has to have the same value as the note it replaces.

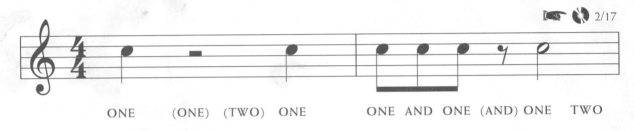

ONE　　(ONE)　(TWO)　ONE　　　ONE　AND　ONE　(AND)　ONE　　TWO

TEST 7

 The following examples contain relatively sophisticated uses of the rest. Count through each piece, tapping out the rhythm or, if you would prefer, playing it through on the instrument of your choice. Pay special attention to the groups of sixteenth notes in exercise three as these are very difficult to count.

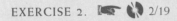 EXERCISE 1. 2/18

EXERCISE 2. 2/19

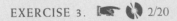 EXERCISE 3. 2/20

PUTTING PITCH AND TIME TOGETHER

So far in this lesson we have concentrated purely on rhythm and ignored the element of pitch. This was necessary, but now it is time to combine our rhythm studies with some melody. This means that not only will you have to work out the rhythm of the piece, you'll also have to find the names of the notes as well.

At the bottom of the page is the music for a tune known the world over as "This Old Man." Begin by figuring out the names of the individual notes—if you really must you can write them on the music itself, although it's a good idea to use a pencil in case you make an error. Figure out the beat value of all of the notes and then tap out the rhythm of the entire tune.

Having done both these things you can now play or sing the piece as a whole. We've made life a little easier by writing the music so that it can be played on the white notes of a piano. ☞ 🎵 2/21

THE NOTES ON THE TREBLE CLEF

It's been a while since we last looked at the notes on the staff. Just in case you are having difficulties remembering them here they are again, but do try to do the final tests over the page without looking at them.

THIS OLD MAN   HE PLAYED ONE

HE PLAYED KNICK KNACK   ON MY DRUM WITH A

KNICK KNACK PAD——DY WHACK   GIVE YOUR DOG A BONE

THIS OLD MAN CAME   ROLL———ING HOME

TEST 8

 Here are five exercises that are designed to test the things we have covered so far. They should be approached in the same way as the other exercises you have done. You may, if you are singing the exercises, experience a certain amount of difficulty due to the lack of a reference note—the key to good sight-reading is an appreciation of the difference between the pitches in relation to each other. In reality, almost any note can be a reference note if you know how to find your way from that note to the notes of the piece. In the following examples use the note of C in the first exercise as a reference note for the other exercises.

TEST 9

Track 2/27 on the CD contains a single bar of music repeated four times. Your task, which is the hardest so far, is to work out which of the four staves shown below matches the music on the CD. Each of the examples shown below is ever so slightly different from the other. You may have to work out the examples first and then play the track on the CD to see which is correct.  2/27

STAFF A.

STAFF B.

STAFF C.

STAFF D.

TEST 10

If you look closely at the two bars of music below you will see that there is something wrong with each of them. See if you can figure out what it is and then try to find a way to correct the problem. (A clue lies in the time signature.)

TIME OUT: SUMMARY OF LESSON 2

Below is a summary of the various points we have covered in this lesson. If there is anything listed below that you are not sure about you should go over it again before going on to lesson 3.

- Quarter-note beats and four-four time
- Half notes and whole notes
- Eighth notes and their subdivisions
- The components of a note
- Dotting a note

- Tied notes
- Rests
- Calculating bar values
- An ability to sight-read simple examples of rhythm and pitch

Scales and Keys

Scales are sequences of related notes. What makes each scale unique is the pattern of intervals that unfolds from the starting note—referred to as the ROOT or TONIC— to that same note played an octave higher. The key of a piece of music is determined by the scale used to construct it.

THE MAJOR SCALE

The major scale is the most commonly used scale of all. If you play the white notes on a piano from C to C you will hear what it sounds like. It doesn't matter if the notes are played in descending or ascending order, the scale still retains its basic properties. From the lowest note to the the highest note, the notes of the scale are referred to as degrees. These can be written out using Roman numerals. If you look at the example at the bottom of the page you will see that each of the eight notes of a C major scale has been assigned a numeral according to its position in the scale.

A piece of music that uses the notes taken from a C major scale is referred to as being IN THE KEY OF C MAJOR.

We use the terms step and half step to refer to the interval between the notes of the scale. If you recall, the half step is the shortest distance between notes in conventional Western music. In this example, the distance between E and F and B and C is in each case a half step. If you look at a piano keyboard, however, you will notice that sometimes the distance between several of the white notes can be two half steps, which is of course a whole step. The interval between C and D is an example of a whole step, as is the distance between D and E, F and G, G and A, and A and B.

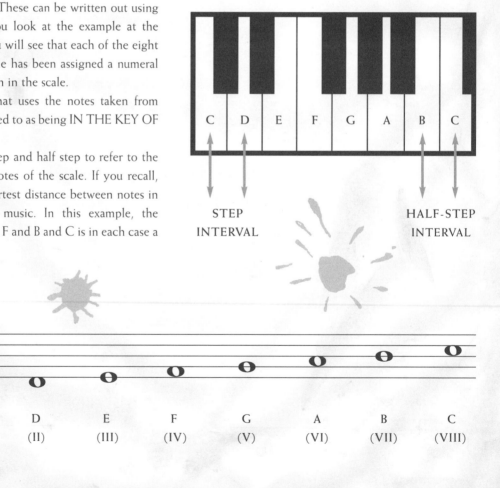

STEP INTERVAL

HALF-STEP INTERVAL

INTERVALS OF THE MAJOR SCALE

The intervals that link together the eight degrees of the C major scale are STEP-STEP-HALF STEP-STEP-STEP-STEP-HALF STEP. It is this set of intervals that defines a major scale and is common to all. Any scale that does NOT have those exact intervals is not going to sound like a major scale.

The C major scale has a sound that can be recognized immediately.

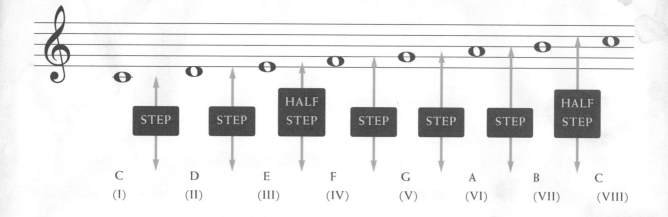

3/1

WHAT'S A TONE?

Some music books use fairly old-fashioned terms such as "TONE" and "SEMITONE" when discussing intervals. While these are still in use in Britain, most other English-speaking countries favor the more commonly accepted "steps" and "half steps," as these also serve as accurate positional descriptions.

THE SCALE OF G MAJOR

The pattern of steps and half steps outlined above can be applied to create a major scale based on any of the 12 different notes of the octave. If we move the tonic from the note of C to the note of G and apply the usual step and half-step pattern, a G major scale will be created. However, because we have moved away from the key of C we will have to start using the black notes in order to maintain the strict step and half-step pattern. In the case of G major this means that we will

have to use the note F sharp if we are to have a whole step between the sixth and seventh notes of the scale; anything less would simply not be a major scale.

While the note of F sharp sounds identical to the note of G flat (it should, it is exactly the same pitch), the context forces us to use F sharp in the notation. This also saves us the trouble of having to write G flat and then G natural every time we move between these two notes, which would be both dull and pointless.

3/2

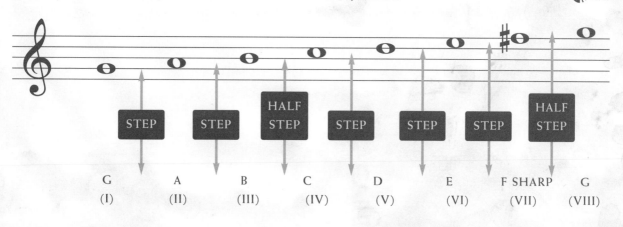

THE SCALE OF F

We can build an F major scale using the usual arrangement of steps and half steps, but this time we will need the note B♭ on the third line. Even though the pitch of both notes is the same, using an A♯ in the second space would be wrong.

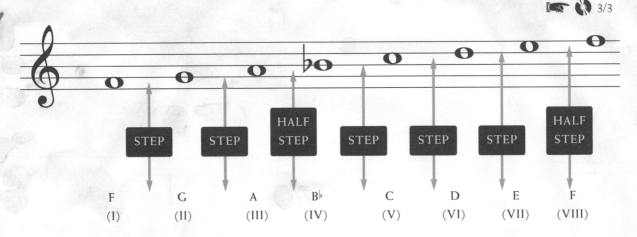

| F (I) | G (II) | A (III) | B♭ (IV) | C (V) | D (VI) | E (VII) | F (VIII) |

KEY SIGNATURES

We have examined the scales of C major, G major and F major. In each case the tonic of the key has provided us with the key signature of the scale. This is not to say that we cannot use other notes in addition to those of the scale, merely that the notes of a particular key remain the same unless otherwise stated. This means that in the key of G, for example, the note of F will always be played sharp unless a natural sign is placed in front of it.

Because the seventh degree of G major is F♯, you could imagine that a piece of music written in G would be littered with sharp symbols if there was not one placed conveniently at the head of the staff. However, because the music has been written in the key of G this means that every note on the fifth line of the staff will be F♯. Clearly, it is much easier to do this and then mark up the exceptions to the rule rather than attempt to do it the other way around. Once this approach becomes familiar to you, you will immediately know that any piece of music with one sharp after the clef is in the key

of G, and also that all references to the note F should be played as F♯. This is also the reason why the note MUST be called F♯ rather than G♭—if it were not, the scale and key of G would have no Fs, but two Gs (G and G♭), each of which would have to be marked as a flat or a natural as and when they occurred (which would be painfully often).

Here is F♯ shown on both treble and bass clefs.

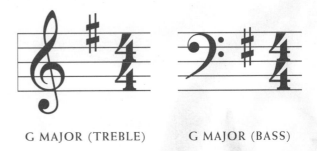

G MAJOR (TREBLE)   G MAJOR (BASS)

Although the key signature marks the sharp on the fifth line of the treble clef, it's actually an instruction to place all F notes as F♯, even those on ledger lines.

G F♯ G A B D   G F♯ E G D B

USING THE FLAT SIGN

The example shown below uses a single flat on the third line to indicate that the music is in the key of F. Every note appearing on the third line of the staff should be played as a B♭, NOT B. Music written in the key of F on the bass clef has the flat symbol on the second line.

 3/5

F MAJOR (TREBLE)   F MAJOR (BASS)

F   B♭   A   B♭   B♭   F   E   D   F   B♭   A   B♭   C   D   B♭

TEST 11

This test is designed to get you ever more familiar with the names of the notes on the staff, a task made all the more difficult by the use of key signatures. Unfortunately, the only way to become truly familiar with the use of key signatures is to practice them repeatedly. Take a look at other pieces of music, perhaps from a library, and see if you can find any that are in the keys we have covered so far.

EXERCISE 1. 3/6

EXERCISE 2. 3/7

EXERCISE 3. 3/8

OTHER KEY SIGNATURES

We have so far looked only at two alternatives to a key signature of C major: G major, which has one sharp (F♯), and F major, which has one flat (B♭). As mentioned earlier, however, so long as we stick to the pattern of intervals that defines a major scale it is possible to create major scales from any starting note.

The time signatures for all of the major scales can be recognized from the number of sharps or flats shown at the beginning of the staff, as you will see shortly. The number of sharps and flats in the key, and their positions on the staff, follows a set, almost mathematical, pattern that is quite logical.

THE SHARPS

The G major scale follows the same pattern of steps and half steps as the key of C but requires the addition of a sharp in order to maintain this pattern. If we continue this process you will begin see the gradual emergence of a clear pattern.

Continuing movements along the fifth degree, the major-scale that begins on the fifth degree of G major will have a tonic—and hence key signature—of D. If you project the major scale intervals shown on page 35 from the note D, you will discover that two sharps are needed to construct the scale correctly. The F♯ from our previous scale is still there, but this time we have

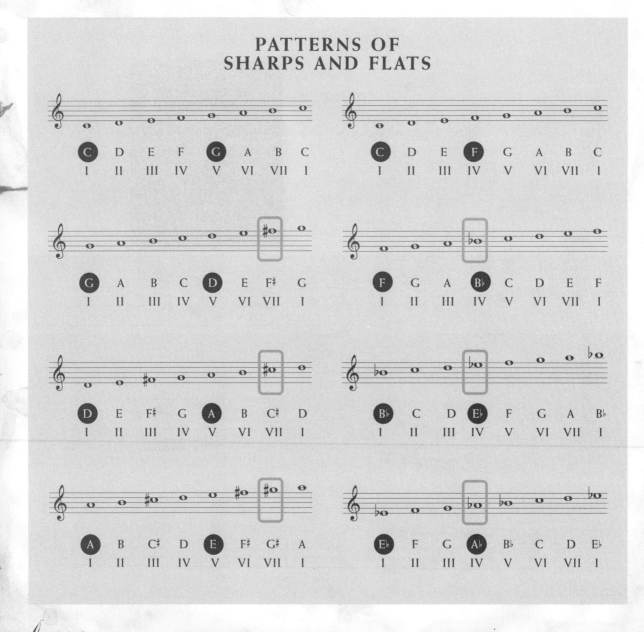

PATTERNS OF
SHARPS AND FLATS

to add a second sharp to make the seventh degree of the new scale work correctly. This means that two sharps F♯, and C♯, are needed for the key signature of D major.

If we go one further we can then begin to build a scale on the fifth degree of our new D scale. The fifth note of the D scale is A, which means that A is our new tonic. This time, however, we will need to use three sharps to build our scale correctly. As before, the sharps from the previous scale can be carried over and a new one added. In this case, as in the others, the new sharp emerges on the seventh note of the scale. This means that the key of A requires the use of F sharp, C sharp, and the new sharp, G sharp.

The process we are following, of adding a sharp to the seventh degree of each new scale built on the fifth degree of another, can be continued over several keys, although in practice rarely cycles beyond the key of F♯, which has six sharps. This relationship is shown on the opposite page in the left-hand column.

THE FLATS

The same patterns can be applied to build up flats in the key signature, except that this time we shall be cycling through on the fourth note of the scale rather than the fifth. This means that in the key of C we build the next scale from the fourth note, which is F. As we have already seen, this requires the use of a B flat in order to maintain the pattern of steps and half steps.

The fourth degree of the F major scale is B flat. If we use the same pattern of intervals from the note B♭, the new scale will be made up from the notes B♭, C, D, E♭, F, G, and A. You can see the same kind of pattern beginning to emerge. A flat is added to the fourth degree of the resulting scale each time a major scale is built from the fourth degree.

If we continue to cycle through in this way we soon discover that the fourth degree of B♭ is E♭. Following the major-scale intervals correctly from E♭ major requires the addition of a flat on the fourth degree, thus the new scale is E♭, F, G, A♭, B♭, C, D, E♭. The relationship between the "flat" scales is shown across the page in the right-hand column in the panel.

Don't worry if all of this seems a little confusing at this stage. We are, after all, dealing with music and not math. You are bound to find in practice that the use of key signatures is not at all a complex problem.

TEST 12

Please answer each of the following:

1. Which major key signature uses no sharps or flats?
2. The key of F uses the note A♯. Is this true?
3. Name the fourth degree of G major.
4. Are there two sharps or three in the key of D major?
5. The interval between the notes E and F could be called a step. Is this true?
6. Which major key uses five sharps?
7. The sixth degree of D major is the same note as the second degree of A major. Is this true?
8. In the key of G major on the bass clef, the sharp symbol appears on the fourth space. Is this true?
9. The first seven notes of this major scale have been jumbled up—E, A, B, C♯, F♯, D, G♯. Put them in sequence and name the scale.
10. Name the seventh degree of A major.
11. Would it always be accurate to describe the interval between the notes G and C as five half steps?
12. How many sharps or flats does the key of A♭ major require?
13. In the key signature of E, the four sharps appear on the same lines on both the treble clef and the bass clef. Is this true?
14. Is the third degree of C major and the sixth degree of G major the same note?
15. F♯ and A♭ have the same pitch. Is this true?
16. Is B♭ the same note as A♯?
17. The major keys of C, G, D, and A all have at least one sharp on the seventh degree. Is this true?
18. How many flats does the key of E♭ require?
19. B♭ major uses two flats. Which are they?
20. The sixth degrees of E♭ and D are one half step apart. Is this true?

THE CIRCLE OF FIFTHS

The CIRCLE OF FIFTHS is sometimes depicted as a wheel. It is a useful way of laying out the relationships that exist between scales starting on the fourth or fifth degrees of the previous scales.

When moving clockwise around the circle of fifths, each new key starts on the fifth degree of the previous scale and adds a sharp at the seventh degree of the new scale. This continues the entire way around the wheel, although in practice most people start to think in terms of flats when they get halfway around the circle. (It takes forever to list all of the sharps in C sharp, and so this key

signature has been omitted from the charts below.)

Moving counterclockwise around the circle produces another pattern. Each new letter is a fifth down from the tonic of the previous scale, which means that the starting note for the new scale will always be built on the fourth degree of the old scale. Moving counterclockwise, this also means that we have to add a flat to the key signature in order to maintain the required pattern of steps and half steps. The fourth degree of the new scale tells us which note will have to be flattened.

Although it might seem a little long-winded, the circle of fourths provides a very useful way to get a feel

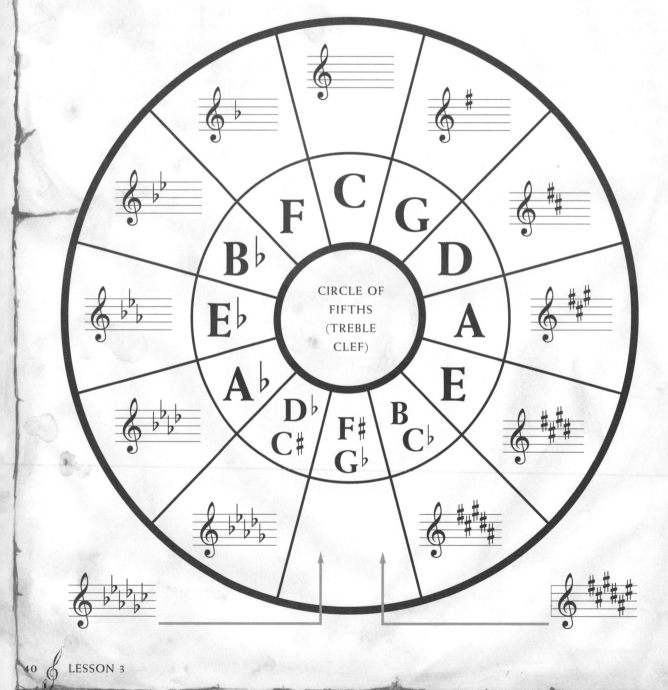

for the way that the key signatures are created and also brings an understanding of the way that one key is related to another.

On the opposite page is the circle of fifths written out for the treble clef. Most people who are familiar with the concept tend to picture this when they think of the circle of fifths. However, you should also acquaint yourself with the circle as it would appear when written out in the bass clef. This is especially true for those who play instruments that tend to be notated in the bass clef. The circle of fifths written in the bass clef is shown below.

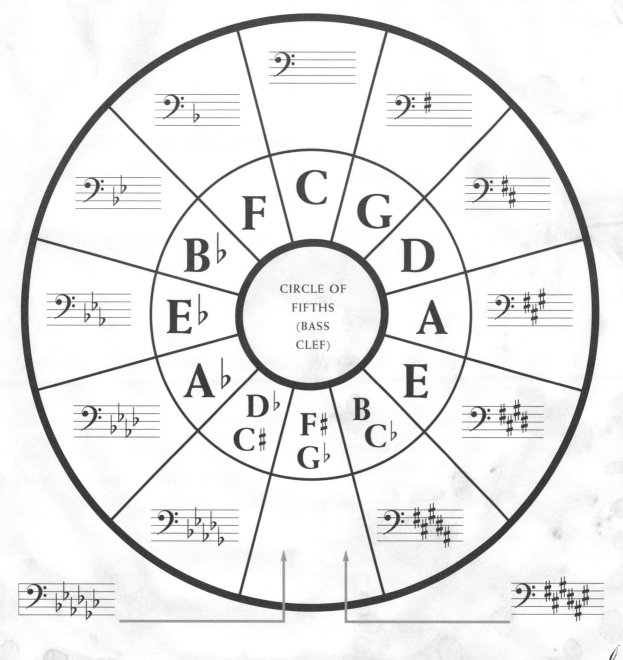

LESSON 4

Time and Tempo

In conventional notation notes are grouped together in regular groupings or clusters called bars. Although the number of notes contained within them may vary enormously, each bar in a piece of music will contain a set number of beats. So far we have dealt exclusively with music built on four beats in the bar. We already know this as four-four time, but of course this is not the only time signature available to us.

TIME SIGNATURES

As we have already seen, four-four time is a very common time signature, so common that it is sometimes referred to as COMMON TIME. Common time is so common, in fact, that it even has its own shorthand symbol. This is a modified C, which looks like this: **C**. It is a throwback to the early days of notation. But, of course, four-four is far from being the only time signature we can use.

Before we go any further, we should take a look at what the fraction-like numbers at the start of a piece of music are really telling us. The number at the bottom of the "fraction" lets us know the time value of each of the beats in a bar. The number on top of that tells us exactly how many of these beats there are in the bar. So far we have looked only at combinations of four quarter beats in a bar. If the bottom number is given as

a two, however, this indicates that the beat has been divided into half beats. If the bottom number is an eight, then clearly the beat has been divided into eighths.

SIMPLE TIME

If you listen to the examples given on the next page you will see that the bars have been divided into two-four, three-four, and four-four. Emphasis has been placed on the first beat of each bar and any effect produced by the time signature shows up in the repeated pulse of the first beat of the bar.

Only one bar of music is shown for each of the examples but on the CD each staff is played for 16 bars, giving you the opportunity to listen and join in. Clap along, counting out the beats, emphasizing the word "ONE" each time. The first example repeats the count <u>ONE</u>-TWO. In the second example the count will be <u>ONE</u>-TWO-THREE. Such accenting naturally occurs every two or three beats—you can think of four-four time as having two accents, the strongest on ONE and a weaker one on THREE.

If these accents were not there the three time signatures would be very difficult to tell apart because the tempo in each case is identical. The word "Tempo" refers, in this instance, to the time taken to play any of the quarter notes that make up the bars. As such, it is also a measure of the overall speed at which the music is played. Although arranged differently, the time taken to play each quarter note is identical.

EACH BAR COMPRISES FOUR BEATS

EACH BEAT IS A QUARTER NOTE

CROTCHETS OR QUARTER NOTES?

As we mentioned earlier, not everyone uses the same terms to describe common elements in music. Europe in particular, with its centuries-old traditions associated with notation, tends to favor the use of archaic Italianate terms such as "semibreve" when referring to a whole note. Similarly, if you are using a European music book you may also come across terms such as "minim", "crotchet," and "quaver." These are nothing to worry about, as they are merely alternative names for the half note, quarter note, and eighth note respectively.

While there is no pressing need to learn these terms right now, it is useful to have a working knowledge of them, especially if you plan to investigate classical music more fully, as much of the literature associated with it tends to use the older, and less clear, terms.

On the right you will find a list of the common note values and their European equivalents.

𝅝
SEMIBREVE (WHOLE NOTE)

𝅗𝅥
MINIM (HALF NOTE)

𝅘𝅥
CROTCHET (QUARTER NOTE)

𝅘𝅥𝅮
QUAVER (EIGHTH NOTE)

𝅘𝅥𝅯
SEMIQUAVER (SIXTEENTH NOTE)

𝅘𝅥𝅰
DEMISEMIQUAVER (THIRTY-SECOND NOTE)

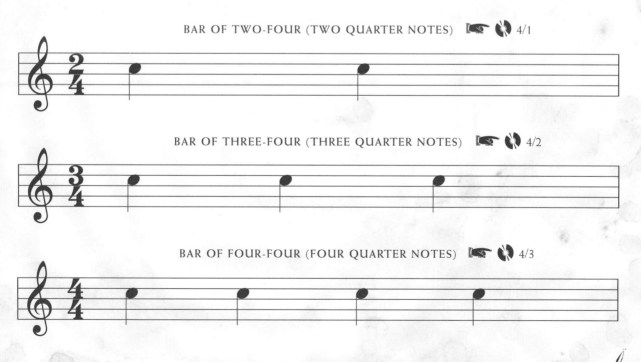

BAR OF TWO-FOUR (TWO QUARTER NOTES) ☞ 🎧 4/1

BAR OF THREE-FOUR (THREE QUARTER NOTES) ☞ 🎧 4/2

BAR OF FOUR-FOUR (FOUR QUARTER NOTES) ☞ 🎧 4/3

USING SIMPLE TIME

It may have occurred to you to wonder what the difference is, if any exists, between two bars of two-four and a bar of four-four. After all, they both add up to the same number of notes so why bother with the distinction?

Perhaps the most common use of two-four time is in marching music, which is designed to keep a large body of people moving in step. For example, soldiers marching on a parade ground will be following a pattern of movement that relies on two simple steps. It makes sense, therefore, to avoid confusion and use music which is divided into bars of two, producing the count "ONE-TWO" or "LEFT-RIGHT." While it would be perfectly possible to write marching music in four-four time, one would have to add accents in order to move the stress points of the bar to the right places.

In four-four time there is a strong emphasis on the first beat of the bar and a much weaker one on the third beat of the bar. Marching music, however, requires a strong first beat and then another strong beat two beats later. This means that a two-four time signature is far better suited to the job. Ultimately, notation is a form of communication and while we can always find another way of saying the same thing it is often easier all round to communicate using the simplest method.

MIXED NOTE VALUES IN SIMPLE TIME

The three staves that we examined on the previous page had one thing in common: the total value of the notes within each bar matches exactly with the figure given for the top number in the time signature.

The example below is the nursery tune "Lavender's Blue," which is a simple piece of music in three-four time. This means that when counting out the note values they MUST total three beats. Hence, unlike a bar of four-four time, a note that lasts for an entire bar CANNOT be a whole note because that is worth four beats. A DOTTED HALF NOTE, which is worth three beats, can be used in its place.

The unmistakable flavour of three-four time is often referred to either as "Waltz Time" or "Triple Time."   ☞ 🎵 4/4

BAR LINES

The piece of music above has two types of bar line in it. The first one is a standard bar line, which is being used to separate the music into groups of three-four time. The final bar line is different. This is known as a "DOUBLE BAR LINE." There are two types of double bar line:

Two vertical lines of regular thickness are used to indicate the end of a definable section within a piece of music. But when a regular bar line is followed by a thicker bar line we know that we have reached the end of a piece of music. Other instructions are often placed at or near bar lines.

COMPOUND TIME

Most of the simple time signatures have beats which are divisible by two, but another kind of time signature has beats which are divisible by three, and is known as compound time.

In compound time, a two-beat bar with a time signature of six-eight would be played as two groups of three eighth notes.

This means that when playing the piece one would "feel" a double pulse in the bar. Similarly, a three-beat bar can be played as three groups of three eighth notes in a time signature of nine-eight, and a four-beat bar can be played as four groups of three eighth notes in a time signature of twelve-eight. Count carefully through each of the three examples of compound time shown below and see if you can "feel" the pulse of the music.

BAR OF SIX-EIGHT (SIX EIGHTH NOTES)   4/5

BAR OF NINE-EIGHT (NINE EIGHTH NOTES)   4/6

BAR OF TWELVE-EIGHT (TWELVE EIGHTH NOTES)   4/7

INTERPRETATION

Music would be deeply dull and two-dimensional were it not for the subtle use of emphasis when playing certain parts of a bar of music. One clue as to the position of the correct points of emphasis can be found in the way the notes are grouped together.

In the example shown directly below, there are two bars of music laid out in 6/8 time. In the first bar the music has been placed in two groups of three. The second bar has the same number of notes but this time they are grouped in sets of two. These groupings tell us

an awful lot about the way the music should be played. The first bar has a strong emphasis on its first beat and a slightly weaker one on the fourth beat of the bar, as indicated by the way the notes are grouped. In the second bar, however, the emphasis remains on the first beat but is followed by a subtle emphasis on both the third and fifth beats. This creates a very different effect on the ears of the listener. However, the strongest differences in dynamics are indicated in an entirely different way, which we shall get to presently.   4/8

ASYMMETRIC TIME

In addition to the time signatures we have looked at there are also a number of less commonly used time signatures. These are not divisible by two or three and are known as ASYMMETRIC time signatures. Most asymmetric time signatures can be counted in fives and sevens, but bars of eleven and thirteen are also used occasionally.

Although these may feel awkward at first, asymmetric time signatures can, and often are, reduced to combinations of two three or four beats in a bar. This means that, for example, seven-eight time can be seen as one group of three followed by one group of four.

FIVE-FOUR TIME

In the example shown immediately below there are two bars of five-four time, each with a bar comprising five

quarter notes. It might be easiest to imagine the first bar as consisting of a group of two followed by a group of three. As we have not used beams to group the notes and show where the emphasis lies, we have instead added accents (the inverted V symbol) above the notes to be stressed. This makes it much easier to "feel" where the emphasis has been placed. Count the bars ONE-two-ONE-two-three/ONE-two-three-ONE-two.

SEVEN-FOUR TIME

The example at the bottom of the page has a time signature of seven-four, which can be viewed as a group of three quarter notes followed by a group of four, or vice versa. From the placing of the accents you will see that the bars should be counted ONE-two-three-ONE-two-three-four, etc.

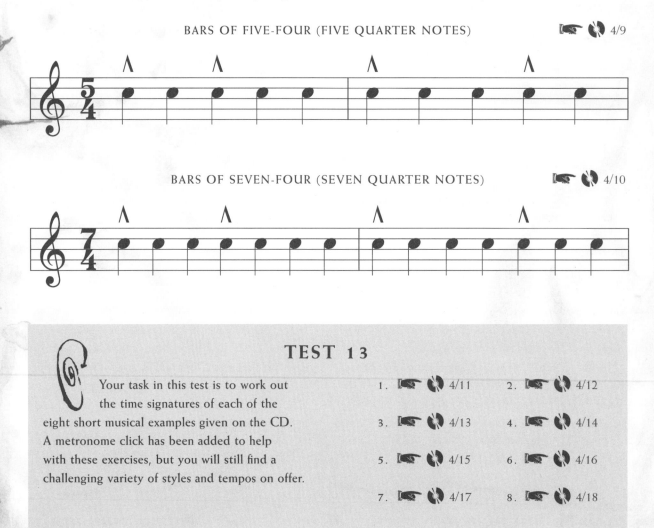

BARS OF FIVE-FOUR (FIVE QUARTER NOTES) 4/9

BARS OF SEVEN-FOUR (SEVEN QUARTER NOTES) 4/10

TEST 13

Your task in this test is to work out the time signatures of each of the eight short musical examples given on the CD. A metronome click has been added to help with these exercises, but you will still find a challenging variety of styles and tempos on offer.

1. 4/11   2. 4/12
3. 4/13   4. 4/14
5. 4/15   6. 4/16
7. 4/17   8. 4/18

TEST 14

 In each of the following eight single bars of music the time signature has been removed from the staff. You should be able to work out the time signature for each bar by totaling the various note values they contain. As an additional challenge, write down the names of all the notes as well as the major key signatures. You can refer to the "circle of fifths" at the end of lesson 3 if you need to refresh your memory.

TIME CHANGES

It is by no means certain that a piece of music will begin and end with the same time signature. Sometimes the composer might wish to change the time signature of a piece of music part of the way through. This is indicated by the simple addition of a new time signature, which may occur at any point on a staff. This means that the music moves, without stopping, to the new time signature and remains there unless otherwise stated. Two changes of time signature are shown below and can be heard on the CD. 4/19

TEMPO

The speed at which a piece of music is played is referred to as the TEMPO. In notation, tempo can be shown in one of two ways. Sometimes you will see a general idea of tempo indicated with the use of words such as "Slow," "Fast," etc. A more accurate alternative is to specify the tempo in terms of beats per minute. This is done by placing a note equal to the value of a single beat followed by a figure.

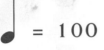

The example above indicates that one hundred quarter-note beats are to be played every minute.

The tempo can be measured in a number of ways. Traditionally, musicians and composers have used a pyramid-shaped mechanical device called a METRONOME. This device, which is based on the pendulum clock, can be set manually so that it provides an audible click at a specified tempo and on each of the beats. Invented in around 1812 by a Dutchman named Dietrich Winkel, the idea of the metronome was copied, modified, and patented in 1815 by Johann Maelzel who, although later sued by Winkel, became the name most commonly associated with the device. So much so, in fact, that it became widely known as the "Maelzel Metronome" and, to the present day, some written music shows the letters "M.M." alongside the time value.

M.M. = 100

Advances in the technology associated with recording music have since given us the electronic drum machine and the MIDI sequencer. Although complex in design, the overall effect is identical, although the terminology has changed. The widespread use of electronic equipment and the growth of "DJ culture" with its accompanying electronic dance music has brought the term "BPM" (beats per minute) into popular usage.

The BPM figure may be adhered to in music, such as dance music, that relies on the use of sequencers but in practice real musicians rarely use the BPM figure as anything more than a general guide, often speeding up or slowing down as the mood of the music dictates. This vague approach to tempo is recognized in the use of the Italian word "circa," meaning "about." This is indicated by a small "c" placed in front of the BPM figure.

CHECKING NOTE VALUES

Most BPM figures are shown in terms of quarter-note values, but these can alter to include half notes or eighth notes depending on the music. If you look at

SIMPLE TO COMPOUND

The notion of attributing a fixed time value to a note type can also be found when a piece of music changes between simple time and compound time, such as between three-four and six-eight. In the example shown below, to keep the tempo consistent it must be shown that the time value of the quarter note in simple time (three-four) is identical to the value of a dotted quarter note in compound time (six-eight). This can be achieved by equating the quarter note and dotted quarter note directly above the bar line at which the change in time signature comes into effect. You can hear the difference this makes on the CD. The first example is played as shown below—the second as if the mark had not been made directly above the bar line.

4/20

TEMPO MARKS

ITALIAN NAME	DESCRIPTION	BPM
GRAVE	VERY SLOW, SERIOUS	BELOW 40
LENTO	SLOW	40–55
ADAGIO	SLOW (LITERALLY, AT EASE)	55–75
ANDANTE	WALKING SPEED	75–105
MODERATO	MODERATE SPEED	105–120
ALLEGRO	FAST (LITERALLY, CHEERFUL)	120–150
VIVACE	LIVELY	150–170
PRESTO	VERY FAST	170–210
PRESTISSIMO	AS FAST AS POSSIBLE	ABOVE 210

the two BPM figures shown below you will see that they look very similar. However, your music would sound very odd if you mixed them up as one specifies one hundred half notes per minute while the other requires two hundred quarter notes per minute.

WRITTEN TEMPO MARKS

For several centuries now classical musicians throughout the world have had to acquaint themselves with a modest vocabulary of foreign, mostly Italian terms. This is because much of the music played by classical musicians has tempo and other instructions which are given in a foreign language.

Shown directly above is a list of the most commonly used of these terms, which are also known as tempo marks. Alongside the translation you will find an approximate range expressed in terms of beats per minute. Clearly, the player or conductor has considerable scope for their own interpretation—a piece played *andante* is likely to sound very different when played at 75 BPM to a performance executed at the relatively brisk 105 BPM.

Tempo marks are not always used simply to indicate the speed at which a piece of music should be played. In times past, composers would also use them to give a general indication of the mood of a piece of music, thereby adding to the general confusion surrounding this issue.

TIME OUT: SUMMARY OF LESSON 4

Here is a summary of the major points shown in this lesson. Because there was so much complex material in this section, you should spend some time reviewing it before going on to lesson 5.

- The components of the time signature
- Two-four simple time
- Three-four simple time
- Four-four simple time
- Compound time
- Emphasis of the beat
- Five-four asymmetric time
- Seven-four asymmetric time
- Metronome marks
- Tempo marks

Minor Scales

As we've already discovered, the major scale, easily the commonest in Western music, is constructed using a fixed pattern of seven intervals. Another set of scales that you are also bound to encounter are the MINOR SCALES. These fall into one of three types, each with a sound of its own. Like the major scale, the minor scales have their own fixed set of seven intervals, which lies between the root and the octave.

SO, WHAT IS A MINOR SCALE?

Each scale type has a sound all of its own. Although it would be foolish to claim that everything written in a major key sounds bright and upbeat, when compared to music written in a minor key this is often the case. For example, "The Wedding March," which is written in a major key, contrasts starkly with "The Funeral March," which is in a minor key. ☞ 🎵 5/1

THE NATURAL MINOR SCALE

The main characteristic of the major scale, aside from its set pattern of intervals, is the fact that these intervals remain fixed. This is not the case for the minor scales, where subtle differences between the arrangement of

the intervals create quite different effects. There are three different types of minor scale: the natural minor (or RELATIVE MINOR); the HARMONIC MINOR; and the MELODIC MINOR. All three differ from the major scale in that the 3rd note is always lowered by a half step. The point at which the minor scales differ from each other occurs on the 6th and 7th notes.

The NATURAL MINOR scale is shown below. As you can see, the intervals are step-half step-step-step-half step-step-step. In many respects the natural minor scale is essentially a major scale with the 3rd, 6th, and 7th notes each lowered by a half step. If you listen to the CD you will hear the scale played both ascending from the root note (as shown below) and descending. ☞ 🎵 5/2

STEP	HALF STEP	STEP	STEP	HALF STEP	STEP	STEP
C	D	E♭	F	G	A♭	B♭	C
(I)	(II)	(III)	(IV)	(V)	(VI)	(VII)	(VIII)

RELATIVE MAJORS AND MINORS

The similarities between the major and natural minor scales become all the more obvious when the natural minor scale is constructed from the sixth note of the major scale. In the example shown below, an A natural minor scale has been constructed from the sixth note of the C major scale. Although the two scales start from different roots, close inspection reveals that they are, in fact, made up of identical notes. The real difference occurs in the sound of the two scales. To hear this, try playing them, or listen to track 5/3 on the CD.

The key of A minor can be described as the RELATIVE MINOR of C major, but equally the key of C major can just as reasonably be described as a RELATIVE MAJOR of A minor.   ☞ 🔊 5/3

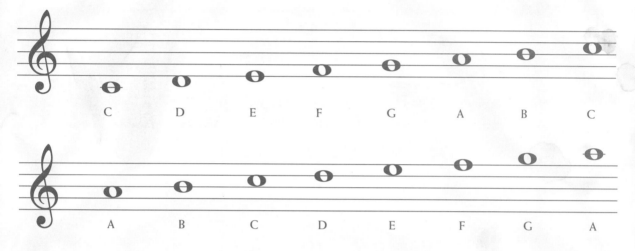

RELATIVE MINOR RELATIONSHIPS AND KEY SIGNATURES

The special relationship between the major and minor scales is enormously useful when attempting to figure out the key signature of a piece of music. Having learned that counting the sharps and flats between the clef and the time signature can tell us the key of a piece of music, the same trick can be used to figure out the key of music based on a minor scale.

Below you will find all of the major-key signatures, denoted by shapes or flats, along with the key signatures of their relative minor "partners".

THE HARMONIC MINOR SCALE

The harmonic minor scale differs from the natural minor scale in that the seventh degree is raised by a half step. The pattern of intervals required to create the harmonic minor scale are STEP-HALF STEP-STEP-STEP-HALF STEP-STEP PLUS HALF STEP-HALF STEP. You will notice that by raising the seventh degree the interval between the sixth and seventh degrees has now grown to three half steps.

If you listen to track 5/4 of the CD you can hear the sound of the C harmonic minor scale (shown below). 5/4

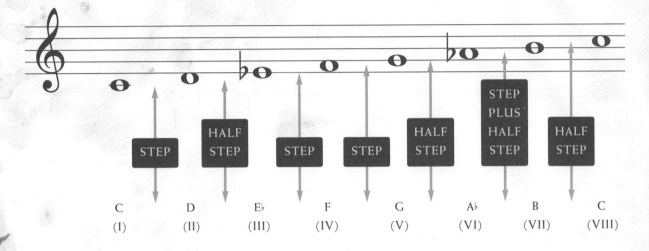

NAMING THE DEGREES

The diatonic scales—the major and minor series—are made of eight individual notes. Each of these degrees has a name. The first note is the TONIC. The fifth degree, after the tonic the most important note in the scale, is called the DOMINANT. The fourth degree is called the SUBDOMINANT, because it shares the same interval as that of the tonic and dominant as counted BENEATH the tonic. The second degree is the SUPERTONIC. This name comes from the Latin word "super," meaning "above," and quite logically it follows the tonic. The third degree is the MEDIANT, so-called because of its position halfway between the tonic and the dominant. The sixth degree is the SUBMEDIANT, which has the same interval as that of the tonic and mediant when counted from beneath the tonic. The seventh degree is the LEADING NOTE.

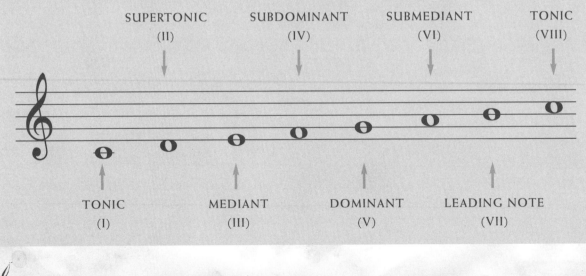

THE MELODIC MINOR SCALE (ASCENDING)

There is a "difficult" pitch interval of three half steps between the sixth and seventh degrees of the harmonic minor scale. The melodic minor scale was created to get around this problem, which it does by raising the submediant (the sixth degree) by a half step to create a more melodious sound.

The pattern of intervals that defines a melodic minor scale is STEP-HALF STEP-STEP-STEP-STEP-STEP-HALF STEP.

You can hear the effect created by raising the 6th degree of the scale if you listen to track 5/5 of the CD. Note the way this scale sounds compared to the C minor harmonic scale shown at the top of the opposite page.

 5/5

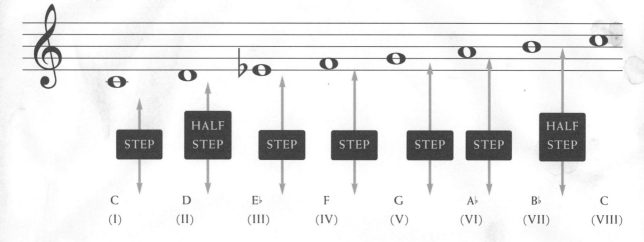

THE MELODIC MINOR SCALE (DESCENDING)

The majority of melodies written in a minor key make use of the raised 6th and 7th notes when ascending—playing UP the scale. Unfortunately, this can sound awkward and unpleasant when traveling back down the scale. There is, however, a simple solution to this problem. When descending the melodic minor scale, play the unsharpened 6th and 7th notes. You will find that these sound far more appropriate. So, while the pattern of intervals described above for the melodic

minor is correct when ascending, when descending you should revert to the notes of the NATURAL MINOR scale. The pattern of intervals for this descending scale is STEP-STEP-HALF STEP-STEP-STEP-HALF STEP-STEP.

You can hear the ascending C melodic minor scale (shown above) on track 5/5 of the CD. This is followed immediately by the corrected descending scale (shown below). Try to get a feel for the way this scale sounds. This is best achieved through repeated listenings. 5/6

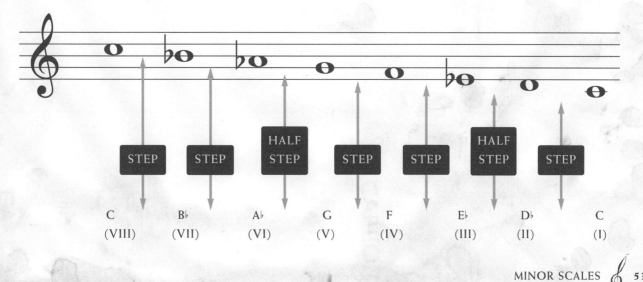

TEST 15

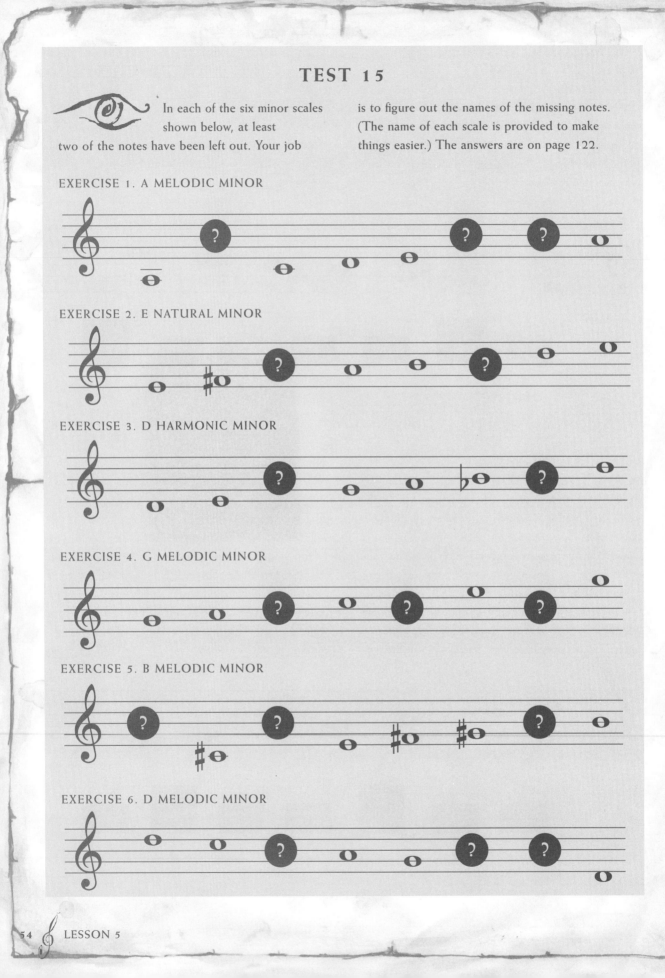

In each of the six minor scales shown below, at least two of the notes have been left out. Your job is to figure out the names of the missing notes. (The name of each scale is provided to make things easier.) The answers are on page 122.

EXERCISE 1. A MELODIC MINOR

EXERCISE 2. E NATURAL MINOR

EXERCISE 3. D HARMONIC MINOR

EXERCISE 4. G MELODIC MINOR

EXERCISE 5. B MELODIC MINOR

EXERCISE 6. D MELODIC MINOR

DOUBLE SHARPS AND FLATS

So far we have seen examples of the use of three of the accidentals—the symbols used to raise or lower pitch. These are the sharp, the flat, and the natural. In some situations, and especially in the case of certain types of minor scale, it may be necessary to sharpen or flatten a note that has already been raised or lowered. This is done with the use of a symbol to denote a double sharp or a double flat.

The double flat is shown in notated music using this symbol—"♭♭." In effect this reduces the pitch of the note by two half steps. A note shown as B♭♭ has the same pitch value as the note A, although it would be

inappropriate to term it "A" in such a context. The double sharp—shown either as "x" or the musical symbol "𝄪"—works in the same way, except that it raises the pitch of the note by two half steps.

The example below shows a G♯ melodic minor scale. The key signature of G♯ minor already features a sharpened F but this scale requires the seventh degree (F♯) to be sharpened. Thus the note is shown as F𝄪. Although the note has the same pitch as G, because we have the key signature of G♯, the "G" space directly above the top line of the staff is already G♯ by default.

You can use either a single sharp or a single flat to restore the note to its original pitch.

TEST 16

Starting at track 5/7 you will hear eight different minor scales being played on the CD in a variety of keys. Your task is to work out if the scale is a natural, harmonic or melodic minor scale. Pay extra-special attention to pitch intervals surrounding the submediant and leading notes (the 6th and 7th notes), as these are the notes that provide the real clues.

1. ☞ 🎵 5/7   2. ☞ 🎵 5/8

3. ☞ 🎵 5/9   4. ☞ 🎵 5/10

5. ☞ 🎵 5/11   6. ☞ 🎵 5/12

7. ☞ 🎵 5/13   8. ☞ 🎵 5/14

TIME OUT: SUMMARY OF LESSON 5

Here is a summary of the major points shown in this lesson.

- The natural minor scale
- Relative majors and relative minors
- Relative minor key signatures
- The harmonic minor scale

- Naming the scale degrees
- The melodic minor scale (ascending)
- The melodic minor scale (descending)
- Double sharps and double flats

LESSON 6

Intervals

The distance between two notes is called the interval. There are two distinct types of interval: when two notes are played simultaneously it is called a HARMONIC INTERVAL; if they are played separately it is called a MELODIC INTERVAL. Some people refer to a harmonic interval as a type of chord, but this is not a strictly correct interpretation.

HEARING INTERVALS

There are three examples of intervals shown on the staves shown below. The top example is that of a harmonic interval which has been constructed from the notes C and a higher-pitched G. The notes are played at the same time. The middle example shows an ascending melodic interval using the same two notes, the lower note (C) followed by the higher-pitched note of G. The bottom example illustrates a descending

melodic interval in which the higher-pitched note is followed by the lower-pitched note of C.

NUMBERING INTERVALS

In lessons 3 and 5 we learned that every scale is made up of a fixed set of intervals from the root and that this remains the same irrespective of the key being used. These intervals can be named by counting from the lowest-pitched note through the degrees of the scale until you reach the highest-pitch note. For example, in the key of G major, the interval between the notes G and A is known as a 2nd (A is the second degree of the G major scale). This, of course, means that the interval between G and B is a 3rd, and so on. When they are written down, these intervals are invariably shown with their numerical value, which means that the examples above would become 2nd and 3rd respectively.

NAMING THE INTERVALS

Within any type of scale the intervals can all be named. Labeling them by the distance between the notes alone is not always sufficient, though. For example, the notes that make up an interval of a 3rd in a G major scale are G and B, but in a G minor scale they are G and B♭. To get around this problem, a prefix is added to describe the "quality" of the relationship between the notes and to provide the interval with an unequivocally unique label. The term "perfect" is used in the major scale to describe the fourth and fifth degrees of the scale (as well as the octave); the other notes in the major scale

HARMONIC 👉 🔊 6/1

ASCENDING MELODIC 👉 🔊 6/2

DESCENDING MELODIC 👉 🔊 6/3

are given the prefixed "major." The interval between G and B♭ is called a MINOR 3rd.

A full set of interval names is shown below for all of the notes that make up the key of C major. Notice also that the abbreviation for the octave, "8ve," has been used in the last example. ☞ 🎵 6/4

C – D	C – E	C – F	C – G	C – A	C – B	C – C
MAJOR	MAJOR	PERFECT	PERFECT	MAJOR	MAJOR	OCTAVE
2ND	3RD	4TH	5TH	6TH	7TH	(8VE)

TRANSPOSING THE INTERVALS

The above example used the C major scale to illustrate the point. However, the names and the relationships between the notes remain the same regardless of the key. In the example shown below, the same relationships are laid out in the key of G major. You will quickly notice that the interval between C and D in the top example is identical to the interval between G and A in the example below. This process is known as transposition and it is possible to transpose the relationship between the notes of a scale to any key, although obviously this will result in a change of key. In this case we have transpose the key from C to G. ☞ 🎵 6/5

G – A	G – B	G – C	G – D	G – E	G – F♯	G – G
MAJOR	MAJOR	PERFECT	PERFECT	MAJOR	MAJOR	OCTAVE
2ND	3RD	4TH	5TH	6TH	7TH	(8VE)

MELODIC INTERVALS

On the staff below, the seven intervals that were shown above harmonically in the key C major have been written down as a sequence of melodic intervals. They are marked as seven distinct pairs. Thus, the first two notes, C and D, make up an ascending major 2nd interval. However, if you now look at the second and third notes, D to C, you will see that they create a descending major 2nd interval. This pattern is followed through to the end of the sequence. You can hear the complete sequence on track 6/6 of the CD. ☞ 🎵 6/6

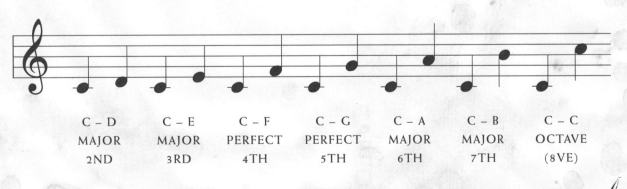

C – D	C – E	C – F	C – G	C – A	C – B	C – C
MAJOR	MAJOR	PERFECT	PERFECT	MAJOR	MAJOR	OCTAVE
2ND	3RD	4TH	5TH	6TH	7TH	(8VE)

AURAL INTERPRETATION OF HARMONIC INTERVALS

Unless you have a well-developed aural sense you may experience some difficulty in recognizing the difference between notes of difference pitches when they are played at the same time. Similarly, you will also have difficulty in predicting how the notes will sound together. This problem becomes all the greater when you are dealing with chords, which may contain three or more notes which are played simultaneously. It is therefore a good idea to get a feel for the sound of intervals. This is best achieved by playing through all of the various interval as groups and also individually as melodic relationships

In the example shown below the first bar contains harmonic intervals, the second melodic intervals. Play through the sequence a few times until you begin to hear the similarities between the two bars. Over time, your aural sense will develop to the point where you will be able to hear combinations of notes and know immediately the relationships that exist between them. 6/7

FROM MELODY TO HARMONY

This example is effectively the reverse of the one shown above. The first bar contains melodic intervals of a major 3rd; the second bar contains harmonic intervals of the same value. Although you should start by slowly playing the notes as a repeated sequence, if you proceed to play the two bars at an increasingly faster tempo the single notes in the first bar will seem to merge together to create the illusion of being played at the same time. Of course, no matter how fast the tempo, the single notes will never—or should never—actually merge fully together but the two different very distinct types of musical effect are worth becoming familiar with. 6/8

INVERTED INTERVALS

Working in the key of C, the interval between the root note C and the dominant note G is known as a perfect 5th. In order for this to be a 5th the note of G must always be higher than the C, However, if we reverse the notes—or "invert the interval"—and raise the note of C by an octave we create a new interval even though we are still using the same two notes. If you look at the interval names for the G major scale shown on the previous page you will see that the interval between the G natural and the higher-pitched C natural is that of a perfect 4th. The notes still make a pleasant sound when played together but the nature of the interval has altered and so too will the sound of the interval. This process is known as an "inversion." 6/9

PERFECT 5TH   PERFECT 4TH
(C TO G)   (G TO C)

TEST 17

 Each of the five following exercises has eight sets of notes arranged as harmonic intervals. Your job is to put a name to each of the intervals shown on the page. We have used a selection of different keys in order to make the exercise more difficult. It is best to start by figuring out the names of the note first. For the purposes of this exercise, treat the bottom note as the tonic note of the root of a major scale and then count through each degree of that scale until you arrive at the note at the top of the interval. This will give you a number that will tell you the name of the interval. All of the test examples are in the major key but you should be aware that exercises 33–40 are written on the bass clef.

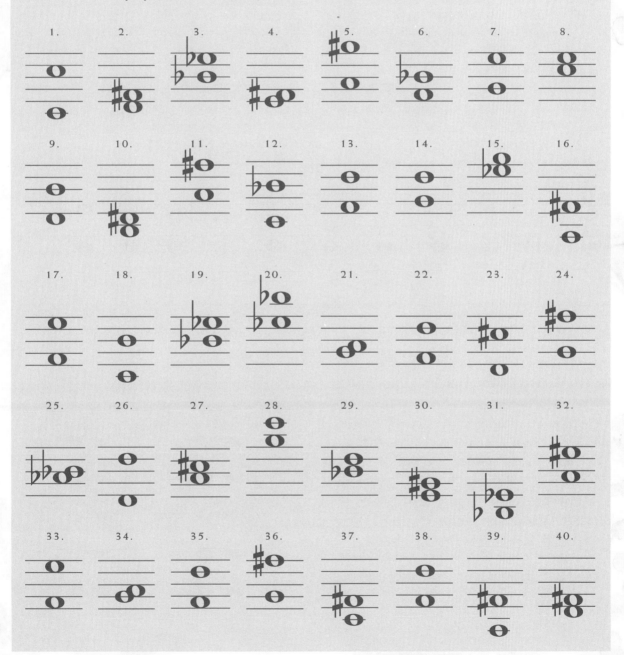

MINOR-SCALE INTERVALS

The notes at the first, second, fourth, fifth, and eighth degrees of the diatonic scales remain the same for all keys. Among the minor keys, however, the third degree is always flattened and the sixth and seventh degrees alter depending on the type of minor scale being used and, when using the melodic minor, whether you are ascending or descending the scale. This means that we need three new labels if we are going to describe the intervals in minor keys. The flattened third, sixth, and seventh degrees become MINOR 3RD, MINOR 6TH, and MINOR 7TH intervals respectively.

The complete set of diatonic intervals is shown on the staff below and a list of the intervals for each degree of all four diatonic scales is shown on the right. 6/10

INTERVAL SET

MAJOR	NATURAL MINOR	HARMONIC MINOR	MELODIC MINOR (ASCENDING)
UNISON	UNISON	UNISON	UNISON
MAJ 2ND	MAJ 2ND	MAJ 2ND	MAJ 2ND
MAJ 3RD	MIN 3RD	MIN 3RD	MIN 3RD
PERF 4TH	PERF 4TH	PERF 4TH	PERF 4TH
PERF 5TH	PERF 5TH	PERF 5TH	PERF 5TH
MAJ 6TH	MIN 6TH	MIN 6TH	MAJ 6TH
MAJ 7TH	MIN 7TH	MAJ 7TH	MAJ 7TH
8VE	8VE	8VE	8VE

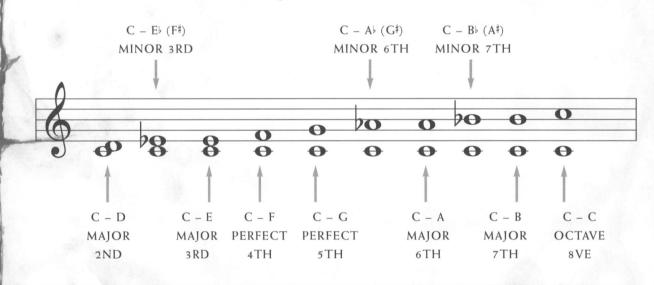

TEST 18

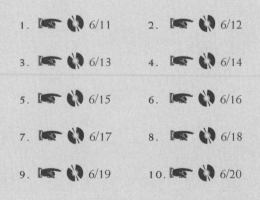

The next 10 exercises on the CD contain different types of interval within the key of C. Your task is to try to name the intervals correctly. This is a very difficult task, so when trying to do it remember that when you hear a harmonic interval, the two notes are played at the same time and that with a melodic interval each note is played separately. Both types of interval are included in the course of this test.

1. ☞ 6/11   2. ☞ 6/12

3. ☞ 6/13   4. ☞ 6/14

5. ☞ 6/15   6. ☞ 6/16

7. ☞ 6/17   8. ☞ 6/18

9. ☞ 6/19   10. ☞ 6/20

CHROMATIC INTERVALS

Chromatic intervals are all those intervals that do not fall under the diatonic umbrella—i.e. those that are not part of the major or minor scales. If you look at the staff across the page you will notice that there are two intervals—C to D♭ and C to F♯—that are not listed. This is because they are chromatic and do not appear in the major or minor scales for the key of C.

The first of these chromatic intervals might be called a minor 2nd. The problem with using this name is that it takes no account of what might happen if the D♭ were substituted for its enharmonic equivalent C♯. Clearly, we could not still call it a minor 2nd. Because the note has been raised by a half step regardless of anything else we can say about it, we instead use a new name. In this case we can describe the interval as AUGMENTED. Similarly, where two notes are of identical pitch, we can say that they are in UNISON. Although the intervals between C and D♭ and C and C♯ produce the same pitches, the relationship is said to be a minor 2nd in the first instance and a unison augmented in the second instance. Generally, the interval between these two notes would be called a "chromatic half step" because the interval from the C and C♯ is not used on any diatonic scale. However, because the interval between C and D♭ does occur in other diatonic keys (A♭ major and the F natural and harmonic minor scales, for example) it is commonly referred to as a "diatonic half step."

Another type of chromatic interval is the DIMINISHED half step, which involves lowering the pitch of the upper note of the interval by a half step. This is, quite obviously, the opposite of an augmented interval.

THE FULL SET

The names used to describe the relationships between intervals are: perfect, major, minor, augmented, and diminished. In effect this gives us the full set of names used for this purpose and any interval, when examined closely, will fall into one of these categories

Intervals with a value of a 2nd, 3rd, 6th, and 7th can be diminished, minor, major or augmented; intervals of a unison, 4th, 5th, and 8ve can only be diminished, perfect or augmented.

SHORTHAND NOTATION FOR INTERVALS

Intervals can, for convenience sake, be notated in shorthand using a variety of different symbols.

A major or perfect interval can be shown as upper-case roman numerals. For example, a major 6th can be notated as "VI."

Minor equivalents are shown in lower-case Roman numerals, thus a minor 3rd can be notated as "iii." Augmented intervals are indicated with a "plus" sign and diminished intervals with a "degree" symbol. Thus, "V+" signifies an augmented 5th and "V°" denotes a diminished 5th.

I – UNISON
II° – DIMINISHED 2ND
II – MINOR 2ND
II – MAJOR 2ND
II – AUGMENTED 2ND
III° – DIMINISHED 3RD
III – MINOR 3RD
III – MAJOR 3RD
III+ – AUGMENTED 3RD
IV° – DIMINISHED 4TH
IV – PERFECT 4TH
IV+ – AUGMENTED 4TH
V° – DIMINISHED 5TH
V – PERFECT 5TH
V+ AUGMENTED 5TH
VI° – DIMINISHED 6TH
VI – MINOR 6TH
VI – MAJOR 6TH
VI+ – AUGMENTED 6TH
VII – DIMINISHED 7TH
VII – MINOR 7TH
VII – MAJOR 7TH
VII+ – AUGMENTED 7TH
VIII (8VE) – OCTAVE

THE FULL RANGE OF INTERVALS

In the table below you will find a full range of interval names for the key of C, with the enharmonic equivalents linked by a line—the augmented 4th between C and F♯ has the same pitch value as the diminished 5th between C and G♭. You should also notice that the double-flat symbol (♭♭) is used here. In the case of the minor 2nd, because the higher note of this interval has already been flattened, diminishing the note adds a further flat.

There *are* other possible intervals within a single octave but these require the introduction of such terms as "doubly augmented" and "doubly diminished" and are rarely ever used.

You can follow these four simple rules to remember the way in which the interval names work:

- Raising a major or perfect interval by a half step will create an AUGMENTED interval.
- Raising a minor interval by a half step creates a MAJOR interval.
- Lowering a perfect or minor interval by a half step creates a DIMINISHED interval.
- Lowering a major interval by a half step creates a MINOR interval.

TEST 19

Your task is to name the intervals for each of the 20 pairs of note names shown below. The answers to this test can be found on page 122.

1. G TO A
2. B TO F♯
3. F♯ TO A
4. B♭ TO G♭
5. D♭ TO C
6. G TO D♯
7. D♯ TO A
8. F TO G♭♭
9. C TO A♭
10. A♭ TO D♭
11. D♭ TO A♭
12. G♭ TO C
13. C TO G♯
14. B♭ TO D♭
15. E♭ TO C
16. A TO B
17. D TO F
18. B TO F
19. F TO B
20. A TO A♭

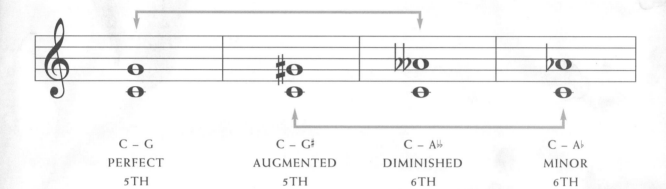

C – G	C – G♯	C – A♭♭	C – A♭
PERFECT	AUGMENTED	DIMINISHED	MINOR
5TH	5TH	6TH	6TH

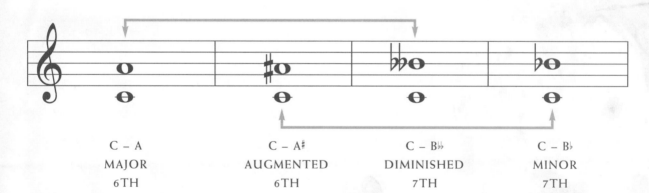

C – A	C – A♯	C – B♭♭	C – B♭
MAJOR	AUGMENTED	DIMINISHED	MINOR
6TH	6TH	7TH	7TH

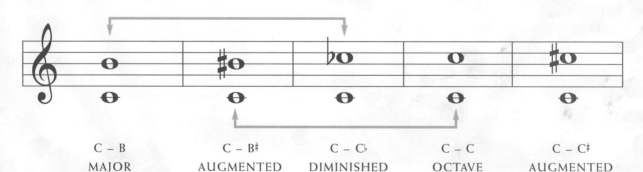

C – B	C – B♯	C – C♭	C – C	C – C♯
MAJOR	AUGMENTED	DIMINISHED	OCTAVE	AUGMENTED
7TH	7TH	OCTAVE	(8VE)	OCTAVE

COMPOUND INTERVALS

Throughout this lesson we have been looking at intervals within a single octave. But it is also possible to extend intervals beyond the octave. These intervals are known as COMPOUND INTERVALS. Naming conventions for these intervals follow exactly the same principles as within the octave, except that you count beyond eight—the octave number. However, simple as this sounds it can cause confusion because the octave note does not take on the original intervalic value plus eight (the number of notes in the octave). Because the octave takes the same note name as the unison, if you count past the octave the first degree you reach is the ninth, which in the key of C is the note D, which is the same note as the second note of the scale. If you continue counting upwards you will reach the 15th, the same note as both the root and the octave.

Regular prefixes are used for compound intervals. This means that just as the interval between C and E is a major 3rd, so the interval between C and E beyond the octave is a major 10th, and remains so.

The staff below shows two octaves of compound intervals and will help you to develop a sense of the way in which chords are constructed.

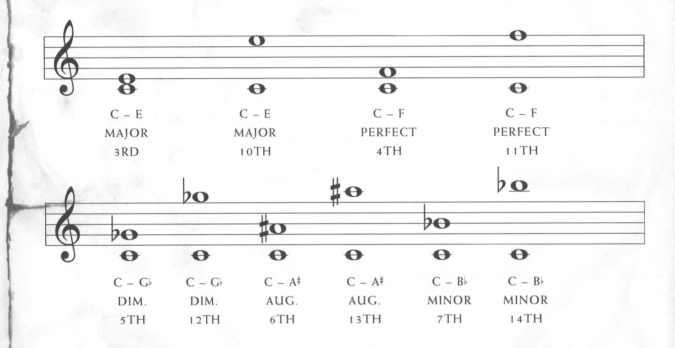

C – E	C – E	C – F	C – F
MAJOR	MAJOR	PERFECT	PERFECT
3RD	10TH	4TH	11TH

C – G♭	C – G♭	C – A♯	C – A♯	C – B♭	C – B♭
DIM.	DIM.	AUG.	AUG.	MINOR	MINOR
5TH	12TH	6TH	13TH	7TH	14TH

TEST 20

See if you can name each of the eight different compound intervals shown below. All of the test examples are on the treble clef.

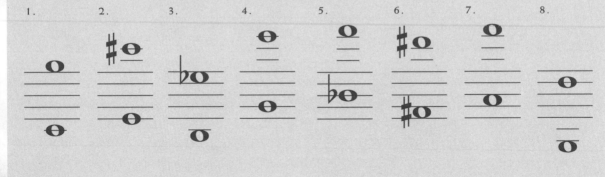

TRANSPOSITION

When a set of notes is moved up or down in pitch as a whole they are said to have been transposed. For this term to be applied correctly, all of the notes will have to have been altered to the same extent. You have already seen an example of transposition in the exercise in which the harmonic intervals in C major were shown to exist also in G major. In this case the sequence of notes were transposed up by a perfect 5th. Any sequence of notes can be transposed up or down by any amount and will retain its characteristics so long as all the notes are transposed by the same amount.

If you look at the first of the two examples shown below you will see that the first staff shows a simple melody written in the key of C. Underneath that staff is another where the same piece of music has been transposed up a major 3rd to the key of E. If you look closely you will see that the relationships between the notes remains identical throughout.

In addition to the harmonic relationships remaining identical, the melodic relationships also follow each other faithfully through the transposition. If you look closely you will see that the first two notes of each sequence are a major 3rd apart.

Both of these pieces are played one after the other on the CD. 6/21

TRANSPOSING DOWN

In addition to transposing upwards it is, of course, just as easy to transpose downwards. The example shown below features the same melody as the examples above but in this instance it has been transposed downwards by a minor 3rd. Once again, if you check the intervals between the notes of all of the examples given on this page you will see that they remain identical.

The transposition of music has very many uses. It can be used to alter the pitch of a piece of music so that it is with the range of the singer's voice. Also, if you are arranging music, you will need to be aware that there are some instruments, such as the trumpet, which automatically transpose—when a trumpeter plays a note written as C, the pitch of sound you hear will be B♭ (see page 100). 6/22

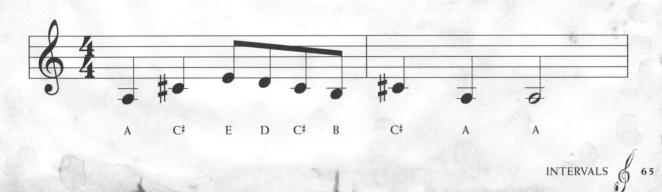

CHANGING KEYS

When an entire piece of music is transposed, the key changes automatically. By moving a piece of music written in C major UP by a major 3rd—as in the example on the previous page—the key is changed from C major to E major. Similarly, by transposing the original sequence DOWN by a minor 3rd, the key changes from C to A major. With the given examples, the new notes were written out in full, but to be strictly correct the key signature should also have changed. This would have been indicated at the beginning of the staff with, in the case of the example that was moved to the key of E major, the addition of four sharps.

If you look at the revised staves below, where the key signature is shown at the beginning of the staff, the accidentals—in these examples, sharps—are no longer needed and will not be shown again throughout the score. The first example is now correctly shown in the key of E major, with its four sharp at the start of the line. The sharp symbols next to the notes of G and F are no longer needed because the key signature tells the player that unless otherwise shown the notes C, D, F, and G are all sharpened. The second example, in A major, is also shown correctly with the addition of three sharps.

Take another look at lesson 4 if this is still confusing.

CONSONANCE AND DISSONANCE

Some harmonic intervals seem to "work" better than others, as you are bound to have discovered as you work your way through this book. The musical terms to describe this kind of effect are <u>CONCORD</u> and <u>DISCORD</u>. These terms have very specific musical meanings but are unfortunately also used rather loosely by many people to describe whether or not they find a piece of music pleasing to the ear.

There are two distinct categories of consonance, although all intervals can be described in terms of being either consonant or dissonant. <u>PERFECT</u> concords are the "perfect"

intervals: unison, perfect 4th, perfect 5th, and octave. <u>IMPERFECT</u> concords are the major and minor 3rd and 6th intervals. All other intervals, including those that are augmented or diminished, are deemed to be dissonant.

Concords and discords are often discussed in terms of their musical "stability." Dissonant intervals are deemed to be unstable in their own right, seemingly requiring that one of the two notes be moved a half step up or down to "resolve" itself. This issue is slightly complicated by the perfect 4th, which can sound dissonant even though it is a perfect concord.

TEST 21

 Transpose the notes in each of the 10 examples shown below, either by a specific interval or into another key depending on what is required (the instruction appears alongside the exercise number). Don't forget to give each of the resulting transpositions a new key signature. This will be determined by the number of sharps or flats it contains.

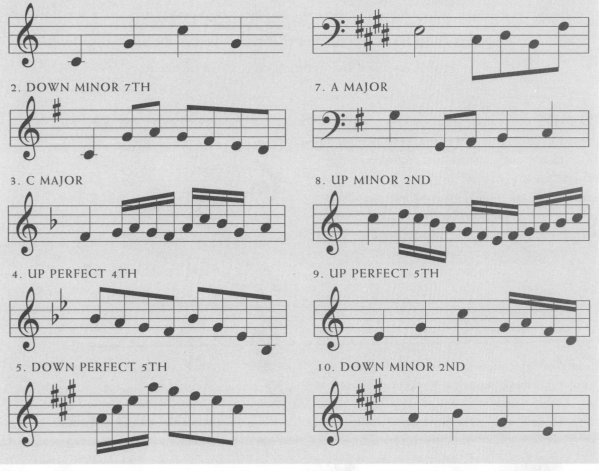

1. UP MAJOR 3RD

2. DOWN MINOR 7TH

3. C MAJOR

4. UP PERFECT 4TH

5. DOWN PERFECT 5TH

6. DOWN MAJOR 3RD

7. A MAJOR

8. UP MINOR 2ND

9. UP PERFECT 5TH

10. DOWN MINOR 2ND

TIME OUT: SUMMARY OF LESSON 6

Here are the major points that we have covered in this lesson. If you are still uncertain about any of the subjects listed review them before you move on to lesson 7.

- Harmonic intervals
- Melodic intervals
- Naming diatonic intervals
- Inverting intervals
- Naming chromatic intervals
- Compound intervals
- Transposition
- Changing key signatures
- Concord
- Discord

LESSON 7

Harmony

The three principle components of music are rhythm, melody, and harmony. We've already covered the basics of rhythm and you should by now be familiar with melody, so that just leaves harmony, perhaps the most interesting aspect of the study of music. Harmony is concerned with pitches that are played at the same time to create chords and add the defining colors to our music.

TRIADS

A triad is the simplest form of chord and gets its name from the fact that it is made up of three notes. These three notes are arranged in a specific sequence of intervals. We start with a root note and then add two other notes a 3rd and a 5th above the root. However, as we have already discovered there are many combinations of these intervals and so each type of chord can only be identified by an examination of these intervals.

The differing qualities of the 3rds and 5ths that can be used to make up triads dictates that there are four different kinds of triads. We will start with the basic major triad, which consists of a root note, another note a major 3rd above that and an extra note a perfect 5th above the root note. In the key of C this would give us the notes C, E, and G. This produces a C major triad, which is commonly called simply C major.

A minor triad is made up of a root note, another note a minor 3rd above that and another note a perfect 5th above the root note. In the key of C the notes we use to form this triad are C, E♭, and G. This produces a C minor triad, which is commonly called C minor.

The diminished triad is made up from the root, minor 3rd, and diminished 5th intervals. In the key of C the notes used to make a C diminished are C, E♭, and G♭.

The augmented triad comprises the root, major 3rd, and augmented 5th intervals. In the key of C the notes used to make a C augmented are C, E, and G♯.

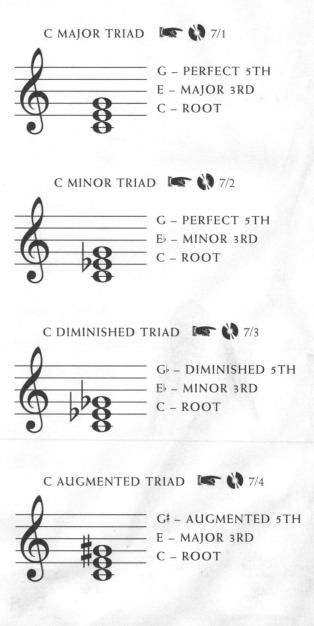

C MAJOR TRIAD 7/1

G – PERFECT 5TH
E – MAJOR 3RD
C – ROOT

C MINOR TRIAD 7/2

G – PERFECT 5TH
E♭ – MINOR 3RD
C – ROOT

C DIMINISHED TRIAD 7/3

G♭ – DIMINISHED 5TH
E♭ – MINOR 3RD
C – ROOT

C AUGMENTED TRIAD 7/4

G♯ – AUGMENTED 5TH
E – MAJOR 3RD
C – ROOT

MAJOR SCALE TRIADS

At the very heart of most Western musical forms is an appreciation of the way that chordal sounds work with each other to create a rich, harmonic landscape. It is the movement of notes within chords that creates these effects and it is an area of study that rewards those who care to put the work in. On the staff below we have written out all of the triads that can be built on a C major diatonic scale.

This amounts to a scale of chords, some major, some minor and, perhaps surprisingly, one diminished chord. The diminished chord is a consequence of the way the major scale works.

Listen to the sequence on the CD or play it on the piano if you can. Listen to the smooth manner in which the triads flow one into another, and notice how satisfactorily the 7th degree (B diminished) is resolved. 7/5

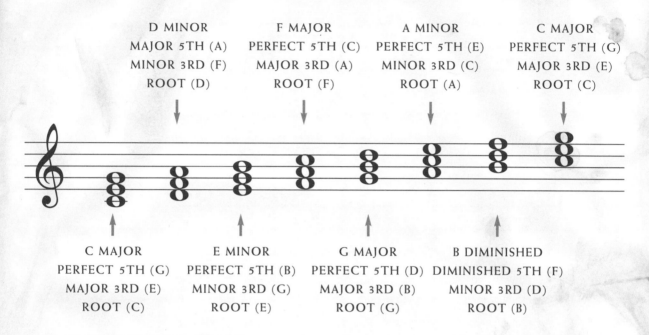

D MINOR	F MAJOR	A MINOR	C MAJOR
MAJOR 5TH (A)	PERFECT 5TH (C)	PERFECT 5TH (E)	PERFECT 5TH (G)
MINOR 3RD (F)	MAJOR 3RD (A)	MINOR 3RD (C)	MAJOR 3RD (E)
ROOT (D)	ROOT (F)	ROOT (A)	ROOT (C)

C MAJOR	E MINOR	G MAJOR	B DIMINISHED
PERFECT 5TH (G)	PERFECT 5TH (B)	PERFECT 5TH (D)	DIMINISHED 5TH (F)
MAJOR 3RD (E)	MINOR 3RD (G)	MAJOR 3RD (B)	MINOR 3RD (D)
ROOT (C)	ROOT (E)	ROOT (G)	ROOT (B)

THE THREE-CHORD TRICK

Convention quite rightly dictates that chords are named for the degree on which they are based. In the above example, C major is on the first degree and so can be called the tonic triad. Similarly, D minor on the second degree is called the supertonic triad (you can refer back to page 52 if you are having difficulty remembering the names of the degrees).

The degrees themselves can also be used as a kind of shorthand description. Thus, in the key of C, a "V" chord is G major—the dominant triad—because it is built from the fifth degree. This approach is sometimes used within informal musical settings where a "one-four-five in G" would mean a chord sequence that uses the following chords from the key of G major: G major ("I"), C major ("IV"), and D major ("V").

As is clear from previous lessons, there is a very special musical relationship between the first, fourth, and fifth degrees—the so-called "perfect intervals." In fact, the "I," "IV," and "V" triads are also termed the primary triads. The importance of this relationship will gradually become even clearer as you progress and gain a greater understanding of harmony. 7/6

| I | II | III | IV | V | VI | VII | I |
| G MAJ | A MIN | B MIN | C MAJ | D MAJ | E MIN | F♯ DIM | G MAJ |

MINOR TRIADS

We can also build triads from the degrees of the minor scale. Unfortunately, because of the differences between the natural, harmonic, and melodic minor scales, the relationships between the degrees is less clear, producing a variety of triads. In fact, tonic triad aside, there are variations on the triads built on every degree of the minor scales.

The chord scale shown below presents the full range of major, minor, diminished, and augmented triads. It can also be heard on track 7/7 of the CD. 7/7

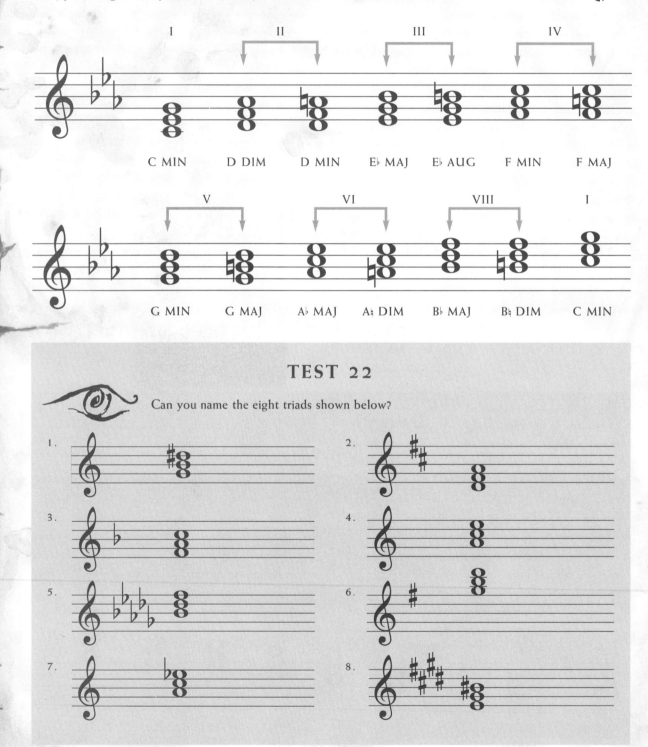

TEST 22

Can you name the eight triads shown below?

PLAYING THE TRIADS

In order to get used to the distinctive sounds made by the four different types of triad you will first need to become familiar with the sound of the intervals between the notes that create the triads. The following set of exercises is a variation on the aural interpretation exercises from lesson 6.

Below are four staves, each containing a different kind of triad in C. The first bar displays the triad as a set of melodic intervals; the second bar plays the notes in their triadic, or chord, form.

By repeating each sequence a few times you will quickly be able to connect the sound made by the melodic intervals with the sound of the triadic chord played at the same time. By treating the four examples as a single sequence of eight bars—they are presented this way on the CD—you will fix the contrasts between each triad in your mind.

The four triads have been shown in C major but in practice both the minor and diminished triads would more likely take a key signature of C minor. 7/8

MAJOR

MINOR

DIMINISHED

AUGMENTED

TEST 23

Each of the next six tracks on the CD is a triad. Simply name the type of triad being played. To make this test slightly more difficult, we have played the triads in a number of different keys.

1. ☞ 🕪 7/9   2. ☞ 🕪 7/10

3. ☞ 🕪 7/11   4. ☞ 🕪 7/12

5. ☞ 🕪 7/13   6. ☞ 🕪 7/14

INVERSIONS

So far we have played all of the triads according to a strict sequence where the root, third, and fifth notes have each been successively higher in pitch. But this need not always be the case. What if, for example, a C major triad was constructed with the root note (C) above both the 3rd and the 5th? As the lowest note is now E, does it shift to the key of E? Of course not: it remains a C major triad. However, if you listen to the two triads played together you will notice that they each have a different emphasis in their sound; they sound the same and yet are somehow different.

By altering the arrangement of the notes within the triad we are creating what is called an inversion. A triad with the 3rd as its lowest pitch is called a first inversion. The same triad can be further rearranged so that the 5th is the lowest in pitch, to produce what is known as a second inversion.

These inversions are shown on the staff below and you can hear them on track 7/15 of the CD. 🐌 🔊 7/15

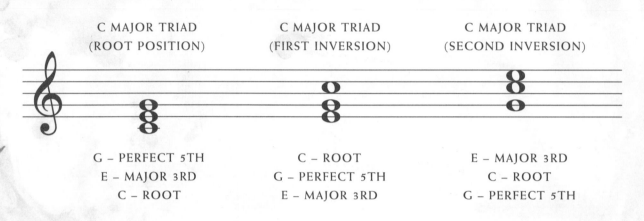

C MAJOR TRIAD (ROOT POSITION)

G – PERFECT 5TH
E – MAJOR 3RD
C – ROOT

C MAJOR TRIAD (FIRST INVERSION)

C – ROOT
G – PERFECT 5TH
E – MAJOR 3RD

C MAJOR TRIAD (SECOND INVERSION)

E – MAJOR 3RD
C – ROOT
G – PERFECT 5TH

INVERSION AND INTERVALS

When triads are inverted, new intervals are created. This can, however, cause confusion for the beginner, not least because surely chords are made up of 3rds? We know, for instance, that C major is made up of a root note (C), a major 3rds (E), and a perfect 5th (G). However, when this chord is inverted so that the note of E is in the bass, the top interval changes. We now have the notes arranged so that the C on top creates an interval of a 4th (G to C). Where does this leave us when it comes to ascribing names to the resulting chords? In truth, when we refer to 3rds and 5ths within any of the four triadic forms we are always referring to the intervals as they stood when they were in root position. An inversion does not change the fundamental nature of the triad.

NAMING THE INVERSIONS

We've already given abbreviated names to the triads formed on the scale. These can be further extended to cover inversions. The roman numerals are suffixed with a lower-case "a" to indicate a root position; "b" to indicate a first inversion; and "c" to indicate a second inversion. Using this system, "IIa" is the root position of the supertonic triad, "IVb" the first inversion of the subdominant triad, and "VIIc" is the second inversion of the leading note triad. These triads are D minor, F major, and B diminished respectively in the key of C major.

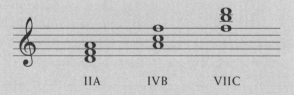

IIA   IVB   VIIC

OPEN POSITION TRIADS

Each of the triads you have seen so far can be referred to as being in the closed position, irrespective of the type of triad being used. A closed position triad is one where all of the notes are grouped as closely as possible to one another. Triads can also be grouped in open positions, where the notes are spaced out so that there is an interval of more than an octave between the highest and lowest.

A root position G major triad with a raised 3rd (B) is not in itself an inversion, although of course the character of the triad will be changed by this action. It is still a root-based triad in the open position because the root remains the lowest-pitched note.

Triads with first and second inversions can be created in the open position. In the second example in G major, the 5th (D) has been raised by an octave, as has the root (G) in the third example. ☞ 🔊 7/16

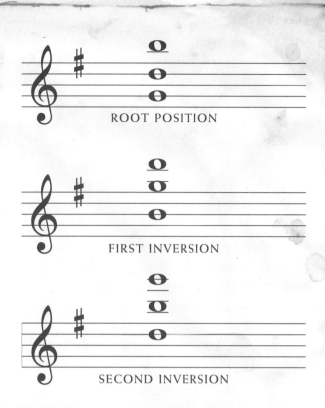

ROOT POSITION

FIRST INVERSION

SECOND INVERSION

TEST 24

Name each of the 10 triads below along with its inversion.

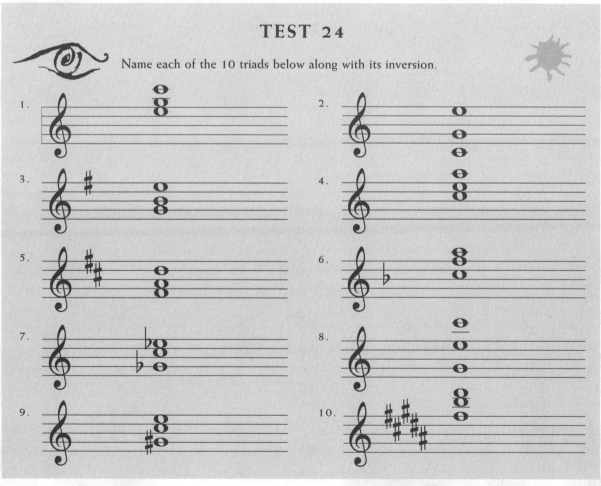

1.
2.
3.
4.
5.
6.
7.
8.
9.
10.

WHAT IS A CHORD?

The simplest type of chord is a triad. Irrespective of its arrangement, it will always remain a triad as long as it comprises just three differently pitched notes.

You have already seen how different musical effects can be created by using the two alternative inversions or using the open position. Unfortunately, this still gives us a relatively limited palette from which to work. If you listen to even the simplest pop music you will be aware of far more complex harmonic activity. This is achieved in two distinct ways: by the addition of repeated notes from the triad in a different register—intervals of one or more octaves—or the addition of one or more notes that could not be said to be part of the original triad.

The addition of a root note one octave below the tonic of the triad is perhaps the simplest development of the basic triad and is certainly one of the commonest. Certainly, the popular music of the past fifty years or so would sound very different were this note not being taken up by a bass instrument such as a bass guitar, double bass or synthesizer.

The example shown on the stave below features a bass note that has been added to the triads on the C major scale. Listen to the effect it has on the overall sound. 7/17

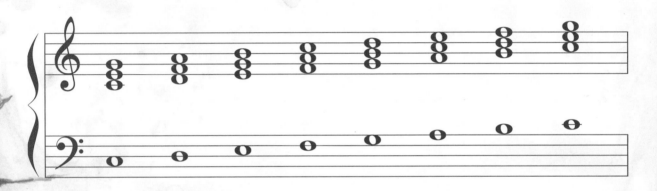

CHORD VOICINGS

The staff shown above features the C major chord, consisting of a root position C major triad with the addition of the note C an octave below the tonic. There are numerous other possibilities for playing such a chord and these many alternatives are known as the "voicings" of the chord.

Contrasts between chord voicings can best be heard on a piano or other polyphonic instruments such as the the guitar, where more than one note can be played at the same time. Monophonic instruments such as saxophones and other brass instruments can only create chords as part of an ensemble.

Different inversions have been used to create the various chord voicings for the G major chord shown below, laid out over two piano staves. The final chord in the sequence is made up from eight notes—the right hand plays the four treble notes; the left hand plays the four bass notes—on a piano, of course. 7/18

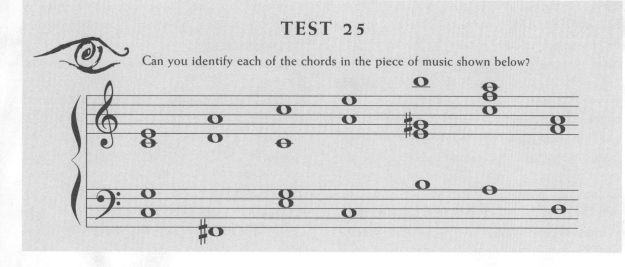

TEST 25

Can you identify each of the chords in the piece of music shown below?

SEVENTH CHORDS

By adding notes from outside of the triad we can create a greater range of harmonic textures than might normally be the case when simply repeating notes of the triad in different ways. The note most commonly added to a chord is the leading note—the 7th. The 7th chord, as it is known, is created in this way.

However, the term "7th note" does not in itself describe a strict pitch within a key. In C, for example, the minor 7th is B♭, the major 7th is B, the diminished 7th is B♭♭ (the same pitch as A), and the augmented 7th is B♯ (the same pitch as C). Depending on the context, it is possible to create several different types of 7th chord. Each of the chords below is a variation on the triads of the C major scale and can be named according to its position. This is abbreviated by its Roman numeral followed by a small 7. The first degree is the tonic and so the addition of a 7th note forms a tonic 7th, or I^7.

7/19

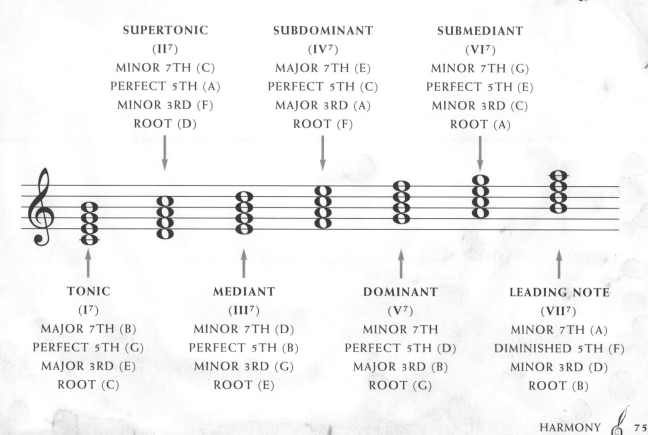

SUPERTONIC
(II⁷)
MINOR 7TH (C)
PERFECT 5TH (A)
MINOR 3RD (F)
ROOT (D)

SUBDOMINANT
(IV⁷)
MAJOR 7TH (E)
PERFECT 5TH (C)
MAJOR 3RD (A)
ROOT (F)

SUBMEDIANT
(VI⁷)
MINOR 7TH (G)
PERFECT 5TH (E)
MINOR 3RD (C)
ROOT (A)

TONIC
(I⁷)
MAJOR 7TH (B)
PERFECT 5TH (G)
MAJOR 3RD (E)
ROOT (C)

MEDIANT
(III⁷)
MINOR 7TH (D)
PERFECT 5TH (B)
MINOR 3RD (G)
ROOT (E)

DOMINANT
(V⁷)
MINOR 7TH
PERFECT 5TH (D)
MAJOR 3RD (B)
ROOT (G)

LEADING NOTE
(VII⁷)
MINOR 7TH (A)
DIMINISHED 5TH (F)
MINOR 3RD (D)
ROOT (B)

THE SEVENTH CHORDS ON THE MAJOR SCALE

By playing through the 7th chords that can be built from the major scale you will become aware of four distinct sounds. Although other types of 7th chord are possible—and we'll get to those later—the four major-scale 7ths are by far the most common.

On the tonic (I) and subtonic (IV) degrees below, a major 7th interval from the root has been added to a major triad. This type of chord is called, not surprisingly, a major 7th.

On the subtonic (II), mediant (III), and submediant (VI) degrees, a minor 7th has been added to a minor triad. Using the same logic as above, this type of chord is called a minor 7th.

On the leading note (VII), a minor 7th interval has been added to a diminished triad, making a half-diminished 7th—so named because the triad is diminished but the 7th is not. A chord where a diminished 7th has been added to a diminished triad also exists, and is called a diminished 7th. The half-diminished 7th chord is sometimes also known as the minor 7th diminished 5th or even a minor seven flat five.

The chord built from the all-important dominant degree (V) is undoubtedly the most important 7th chord of all. This chord requires the addition of a minor 7th to a major triad. Although strictly known as the dominant 7th chord, its use is so frequent that any unspecified reference to a "7th" chord will be taken to mean a dominant 7th.

By playing or listening to this set of 7th chords played with the same root note you will begin to get a feel for them.

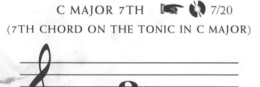

C MAJOR 7TH 7/20
(7TH CHORD ON THE TONIC IN C MAJOR)

C DOMINANT 7TH 7/21
(7TH CHORD ON THE DOMINANT IN F MAJOR)

C MINOR 7TH 7/22
(7TH CHORD ON THE TONIC IN C MINOR)

C HALF-DIMINISHED 7TH 7/23
(7TH CHORD ON THE LEADING NOTE IN D♭)

TEST 26

This test follows on from the chords played above and will help you to become familiar with the contrasting sounds of the various 7th chords. Try to identify whether the chord you hear is a major, minor, dominant or half-diminished 7th on each of the eight tracks of the CD.

1. 7/24   2. 7/25

3. 7/26   4. 7/27

5. 7/28   6. 7/29

7. 7/30   8. 7/31

CHORD INVERSIONS

Inversion names given to major and minor chords are identical to their triadic equivalent. Where the root is the lowest note the chord is in root position ("a"); if the 3rd is the lowest note then the chord is in first inversion ("b"); and if the 5th is the lowest note then the chord is in second inversion ("c"). Things become slightly more complicated when a note from outside the triad is added. If a 7th note is added as the lowest note, then the chord is said to be in its third inversion and is marked with a lower-case "d." Below are the four inversions of a C dominant 7th chord.

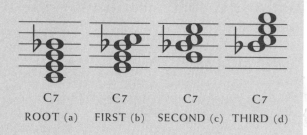

| C7 | C7 | C7 | C7 |
| ROOT (a) | FIRST (b) | SECOND (c) | THIRD (d) |

SEVENTHS ON THE MINOR SCALES

By adding the 7th note to triads built on the natural minor scale we can create the same set of 7th chords that will be produced from a major scale. You may remember that the natural minor scale is also known as the relative minor scale, and that there is relative minor chord for every major chord (see page 51). Because A minor is the relative minor key of C major, the 7th chords built on the A natural minor scale will be the same as those used by C major, although their relative positions will, of course, differ. This means that the sequence for A natural minor is A minor 7th (I), B half-diminished 7th (II), C major 7th (III), D minor 7 (IV), E minor 7 (V), F major 7 (VI), and G 7th (VII).

Three alternative 7th chords can also be created by adding 7th notes to the triads built from the harmonic minor scale. These 7ths, built from the I, III, and VII

degrees, are less commonly used than those shown across the page. Their practical use may be fairly limited—indeed, if they are not used carefully they can sound very strange indeed.

The minor/major 7th shown on the tonic (I) below has been created by adding a major 7th interval to a minor triad.

The major 7th augmented 5th appears on the mediant (III) and is an augmented triad with an added major 7th—although the interval that has been added is, strictly speaking, an augmented major 7th. It is sometimes informally called a major 7 sharp 5.

The diminished 7th rests on the leading note (VII), adding a diminished 7th to a diminished triad.

Play the complete natural minor sequence shown below to hear how these new 7th chords sound. 7/32

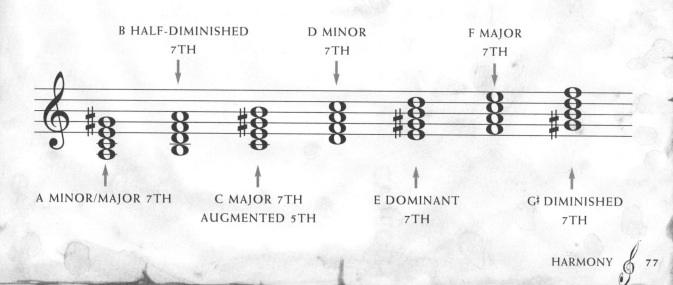

THE SIXTH

We have already seen how the 1st, 3rd, 5th, and 7th notes can be used to create chords. But we can also use the other three notes from the scale—the 2nd, 4th, and 6th—to produce chords.

Adding the major 6th to a major triad creates a 6th chord. A minor 6th chord can be created by adding the same note to a minor triad.

THE SECOND

There isn't really any such thing as a "2nd" chord as it is almost always the compound equivalent of the 2nd—the 9th—that is used. Adding the 9th note to a triad creates what is known as an added 9th chord. This should not be confused with the real 9th chord, which we'll get to in a minute. Often, the added 9th chord is played without the use of the 3rd.

The 9th note can also be added to a minor triad to produce a chord known as a minor added 9th. The interval between the 2nd (9th) note and the flattened 3rd note of this chord is a minor 2nd (or half step), making it a dissonant interval. Although this may seem very odd indeed, these chords are actually widely used.

Chords that have a 9th added to a triad are usually abbreviated to "add nines," regardless of type.

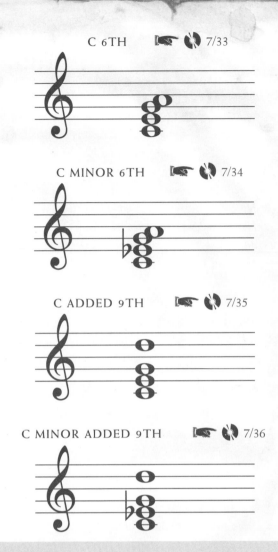

ABBREVIATED CHORD NAMES

More often than not all a musician has to work from is a set of chords that can be played in almost any way. This is usually because the harmony has been laid out in the simplest possible form. It is especially common for the chords simply to be written out on a chart using abbreviated names, which are very rarely backed up by notation on a musical staff. In the next column you will find a list of the most commonly used chords along with their "shorthand" names. The note of C is the root in every example given.

C MAJOR	C MAJ OR C
C MINOR	C MIN OR Cm
C DOMINANT 7TH	C7
C MINOR 7TH	C MIN 7 OR Cm7
C MAJOR 7TH	C MAJ 7 OR CΔ7
C HALF-DIMINISHED	C MIN 7-5 OR Cm7-5
C DIMINISHED	C DIM OR C°
C AUGMENTED	C AUG OR C+
C SUSPENDED 4TH	C SUS OR C SUS 4
C 6TH	C6
C MINOR 6TH	C MIN 6 OR Cm6
C ADDED 9TH	C ADD 9
C 9TH	C9
C 11	C11
C 13	C13

THE FOURTH

The uses of the 4th in chordal harmony are quite limited but very effective. Although used regularly, 4ths are not added to the triad as such but function in the role of temporary replacement, almost always for the 3rd of the chord. For example, in the key of C major, the notes C (I), F (IV), and G (V) are used. This effect creates what is referred to as a suspended 4th chord. Such chords are are usually abbreviated to "sus 4," which is added after the note name of the chord.

A very common form of the suspended chord uses the same movement between the 3rd note to the 4th note in a dominant 7th chord. This effect is known as a 7th suspended 4th chord, or "7 sus 4." They are sometimes abbreviated as simply "7+4."

Suspended 4th chords can be heard in all forms of music. The underlying tension in the chord is usually resolved by moving the 4th note back to the 3rd note at the end of a musical phrase. On the staff below the suspended notes are returned to the major 3rd. This creates a major triad in the first instance and a dominant 7th chord in the second. ☞ 💿 7/37

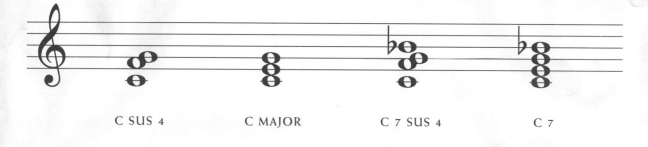

C SUS 4   C MAJOR   C 7 SUS 4   C 7

EXTENDED CHORDS

A wide variety of full-sounding voicings can be created with the addition of 9th, 11th, and 13th intervals. The use of compound intervals in this way is fairly common and the results are known as extended chords.

Ninth chords are so named because they involve the addition of a compound interval of a 9th (a 2nd plus an octave) to a 7th chord. Just as there is a variety of 7th chords, there is also a range of 9ths. The most common—simply known as a "9th"—requires the addition of the ninth note to a dominant 7th chord. Adding the same note to minor 7th and major 7th chords respectively produces the two other commonly used forms of this group, which are the minor and major 9ths.

The 11th and 13th notes work in exactly the same way. Eleventh chords require the addition of the perfect 4th note above the octave to a 9th chord; 13th chords require the addition to the 11th of a major 6th above the octave.

When played in its fullest form, a 9th chord will comprise five notes; the 11th has six notes; and the 13th has seven notes. However, it isn't essential that all of the notes are played.

C 9TH   ☞ 💿 7/38

C 11TH   ☞ 💿 7/39

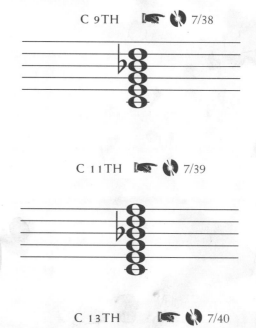

C 13TH   ☞ 💿 7/40

USING THE BASS NOTES

By taking the basic triads and inverting the notes within them it is possible to create all manner of effects. This fact has been exploited to the full in very many different kinds of music, from the very cutting edge of contemporary classical music to much of what can be found in the popular charts.

We will now begin to look at the ways in which the sound of a chord can be altered by changing its bass note, i.e. by switching to a note other than the root. By using other notes from the chord in this way we are effectively inverting them, although informal chord abbreviations usually notate simply the chord name followed by a stroke and then the bass note. For example, the second chord shown below indicates a G major chord is being played over a bass note of B and is notated as "G/B."

Four simple G major triads are shown below being played over bass notes taken from the triad itself, although played in a lower register. ☞ 🔊 7/41

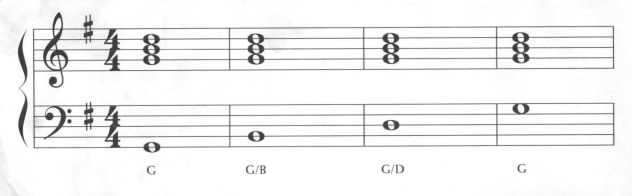

G   G/B   G/D   G

POLYTONAL EFFECTS

A polytonal chord, which is often called a "polychord," is created when two different chords are played together. If you take a C major triad (C-E-G) and play it with a G major triad (G-B-D), the result is the combination of C-E-G-B-D. This is also known as the C major 9th chord.

Polytonal effects can be created by playing chords which add bass notes from outside of the triads. These are not strictly polychords because they use only the root notes.

Five commonly used chords with altered bass notes are shown on the staff below. To make comparisons easier, the bass note is the same in each case. However, the notes of each successive triad differ in relation to this bass note.

The chords below are labeled as triads with a bass note specified after the stroke but they can also be given new chord names based on the notes of the triad in relation to the bass notes. For example, D major (D-F♯-A) played over C when viewed as a C chord is made from the notes C (1st), D (major 2nd/9th), F♯ (augmented 4th), and A (major 6th), making it a C 6/9+4 chord. There are five altered-bass chords shown on the staff below. ☞ 🔊 7/42

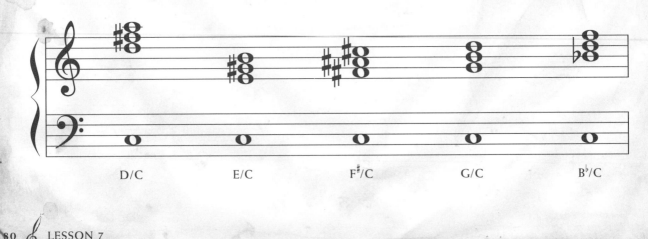

D/C   E/C   F♯/C   G/C   B♭/C

ARPEGGIOS

Back on page 71 we looked at breaking down triads into their component parts. This is the basis of a widely used playing effect known as an "arpeggio". An arpeggio is an instruction to play a chord as a very rapid succession of notes. (Perhaps a clue to the way the effect sounds is in its name, which derives from the Italian word for harp.)

Arpeggio can be indicated in several different ways, three of which are shown on the right. Beneath them is the effect written out in full.

BROKEN CHORDS

The broken chord is very similar in effect to the arpeggio, with the notes played as a rhythmic pattern. Pianists frequently use broken chords when providing accompaniment to other players or singers.

The best-known musical use of broken chords is in what is called the "Alberti Bass." It was popularized by the 18th-century Italian composer Domenico Alberti

(1710-40), and its most famous use is in Mozart's "Piano Sonata in C Major (K.545)." This very specific pattern breaks a triad into single notes, which are then played in the sequence 1st note, 5th note, 3rd note, and 5th note again.

The Alberti Bass on the first staff below is clearly derived from the chords shown on the second staff.

TIME OUT: SUMMARY OF LESSON 7

Here is a summary of the major points of this lesson.

- Major, minor, diminished, and augmented triads
- Triads on the major and minor scales
- Inverting triads
- The open and closed position
- Chords and their inversions

- Constructing 7th chords
- Adding the 2nd, 4th, and 6th notes
- Extending chords using the 9th, 11th, and 13th notes
- Altered bass notes and polychords
- Arpeggios and broken chords

LESSON 8

Phrases and Groups

Part of the key to developing good sight-reading skills is the ability to recognize the patterns that tend to occur regularly in written music. In much the same way as the written word is read not syllable by syllable but as patterns of letters, so the regular rhythmic grouping of notes and phrases can become instantly recognizable after sufficient practice. So let's look at how these phrases and groups are arranged.

USING THE BEAM

We have already looked at the ways in which a beam or a tie can be used to group notes together, but in case you've forgotten, the two staves on the right represent the same set of note values. Clearly the beamed version is easier to read and provides a convenient grouping for the notes. Beaming can also be used even when the notes within the group are of different values.

TRIPLETS

So far all of the examples we have dealt with have involved a subdivision of notes based on a factor of two. By this we mean that they can be halved, quartered, and so on. A beat can also, however, be divided into three equal parts, with the result that the beats are known as triplets. Triplets can be used with any type of note.

Triplets can be notated using one of several different methods. The examples shown on the right are all equally valid (and can be used on a range of note values). Their use is largely dictated by personal preference, but in each case they operate in exactly the same way. In the example immediately to the right, the instruction is for the three quarter notes to be played in the same amount of time that it takes to play a half note. On the CD you can hear the effect of a triplet chord played over a metronome beat. ☞ 🎧 8/1

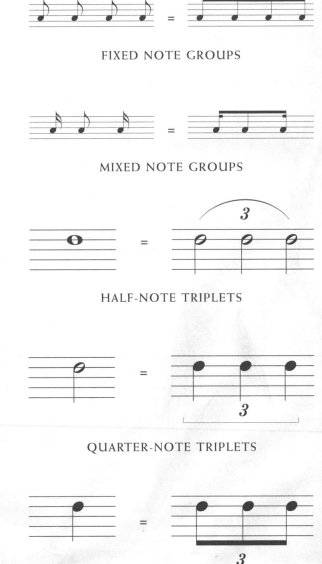

FIXED NOTE GROUPS

MIXED NOTE GROUPS

HALF-NOTE TRIPLETS

QUARTER-NOTE TRIPLETS

EIGHTH-NOTE TRIPLETS

GROUPING TRIPLETS

A triplet division does not necessarily mean that three notes of equal value will be produced, although this tends to be the way they are used. Groups of mixed triplets can be made up from notes and rests of different values. There are four different examples of this shown on the right.

The number "3" is sometimes dropped from the score if there has been an extensive use of triplets throughout. Such a heavy use of triplets would be quite unusual within a simple time signature. Most people would prefer to write the music out in the equivalent compound time signature. If you listen to the example below you cannot fail to notice that despite differences

in notation, the two patterns sound identical even though one bar is in four-four time and the other in twelve-eight.

👈 🎧 8/2

IRREGULAR DIVISIONS

As we mentioned earlier, divisions other than two and three are possible. In the examples on the right a quarter note has been subdivided into: triplets (3), quintuplets (5), sextuplets (6), septuplets (7), and nonuplets (9). While it is possible to divide beyond nine, thankfully this is very rarely needed (and certainly not in this tutor). Pay special attention to the note values that are attributed to each group: divisions of three are treated as if they were divisions of two (hence they are eighth notes); divisions of five, six, and seven take the same note values as divisions of four (sixteenth notes); divisions of nine take the same note values as if they were divisions of eight.

CUTTING TIES

As you will by now have noticed, there are any number of ways in which the same patterns can be notated on a staff. Any system that gets the information across accurately and unambiguously should be considered valid as the function of written music to communicate the composer's or arranger's idea to the performer. Clearly though, some notation techniques work better than others in this respect.

The golden rule when grouping notes together is to avoid too extensive a use of ties. Although absolutely essential when sustaining notes across bar lines, if they are overused within bars the music can become confusing and clearly we are trying to avoid confusion at all costs. For example, using a tie between a half note and a quarter note instead of dotting the half note (which *is* an alternative that any sight-reader would be able to understand) makes the score more difficult to read.

MAINTAINING CLARITY

Ties within a bar can be avoided by using dotted notes in most cases. Below are several examples of how, and how not, to arrange notes in a bar. The desirable version is shown on the right.

STANDARD PRACTICE

When beaming eighth notes and lower there are a set of rules that should be followed. Ordinarily, eighth notes should be beamed either in groups of two, four or, in three-four time, six. This means that the entire bar can be beamed in a two-four or three-four bar of eighth notes. It is best to avoid beaming groups of three eighth notes in three-four time unless they are triplets—which implies the compound time of six-eight. Standard practice is to pull one of the eighth notes out of the group, leaving a pair that play on the beat (see above right). In four-four time you should think of the bar as being divided into a pair of two-beat units. Beaming cannot take place across that divide.

Four eighth notes in the middle of a bar should be shown as two pairs of two rather than beamed (see below). Values less than an eighth note can be beamed on the beat or the half-beat. This means that in four-four time there should never be more than four sixteenth notes grouped. However, eight thirty-second notes would be considered to be acceptable in this instance.

BAD   BETTER

TEST 27

If you look at the piece of music below you will see that although it "works" (with the exception of one serious error) there are a number of ways in which the notation could be improved. This exercise has been deliberately written in an difficult key. As you rework the notation, mark down the note names but don't forget that only practice will make you a better sight-reader.

GROUPING RESTS

Even rests observe a protocol when it comes to placing them in groups. The golden rule is that the rests should be positioned on the beat whenever possible. In a bar of two-four whose only note is an eighth beat on the last half-beat, for example, the first beat of the bar should be a quarter-note rest if only for the sake of clarity. An eighth-note rest can be used to make up the rest of the bar.

On the right are two "undesirable" alternative ways of laying out rests in a bar followed by the "desirable" option. The top example begins with a half-beat rest followed by a whole-beat rest, clearly not ideal because the rests cut across the beats—the whole-beat rest begins on the half-beat and ends on another half beat.

Option two shows a dotted rest —like dotted notes, all of the rests may have their value increased by half in the same manner. The final example shows the desirable way to group rests in a bar of this type.

UNDESIRABLE

UNDESIRABLE

DESIRABLE

PHRASING IN MUSIC

As mentioned in the introduction to this chapter, just as speech can be broken down into self-contained sentences, words, and syllables, so too can a piece of music be broken down into a phrase, which is the musical equivalent of a sentence.

Just what actually constitutes a phrase has not really been defined. If we take, for example, the first four bars of the children's song "London Bridge Is Falling Down," (shown below) the bars shown would constitute a phrase; it could also be argued that the first two bars are also a phrase. 8/3

ACHIEVING BALANCE

If you have looked closely at a lot of music you will see that quite often there appear to be bars of incorrect length. This occurs because not all music begins on the first beat of the bar. The song "Clementine," which is shown below, begins with the first two notes starting on the final beat of the bar. How can it be correct for a bar of three-four time to contain note values that do not total three beats? How can we resist the urge to place a pair of quarter-note rests on beats one and two? Well, in both cases this would be unnecessary, as the beat values are eventually balanced out over the entire piece of music. You may notice that the final bar contains a half note worth two beats,

which complements the single beat that occurred at the beginning of the music. This song has a number of other verses which will also begin on what could be seen as the final beat of the final bar. In fact, if the final bar contained a dotted half note (or a half note and quarter-note rest) an extra beat would be added between verses, which would be wrong. The first line of the song constitutes a phrase in its own right, something which commonly occurs in popular music and just about every other song-based music. It remains perfectly balanced in terms of the time values even though the phrase doesn't begin or end on the bar. 8/4

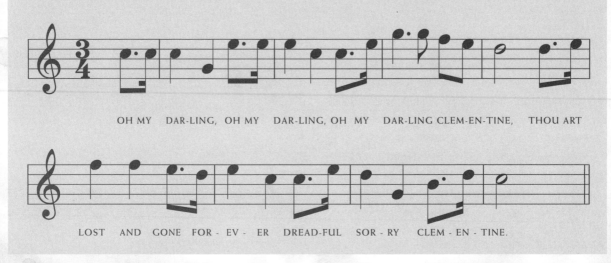

OH MY DAR-LING, OH MY DAR-LING, OH MY DAR-LING CLEM-EN-TINE, THOU ART

LOST AND GONE FOR-EV-ER DREAD-FUL SOR-RY CLEM-EN-TINE.

ARTICULATION MARKS

The way in which a piece of music is performed is often dictated, to a certain extent, by the musical phrases within it. Phrases can be indicated using articulation marks, of which a symbol called a "slur" is perhaps the most useful. It is a curved line which is not dissimilar in appearance to a tie that can be placed around a phrase of any length, regardless of the number of notes or even bars it contains.

The end of a phrase is often indicated by the very briefest of pauses. The same thing occurs in everyday speech, with confusion occurring when people fail to pause at the end of their phrases. It is the same in written music. A slur placed around a phrase has the practical effect of shortening the final note. This emphasizing of the self-contained nature of the grouping tends to help to reinforce its boundaries.

In the examples shown below, the upper staff has three slurs, each of which ends on an eighth note. The lower staff features slurs which end on a sixteenth note and a sixteenth-note rest, which creates the effect of a natural pause.

Within the boundaries of a slur one should always attempt to play the notes in a smooth and flowing manner. This creates cohesion and helps to emphasize the "completeness" of the phrase. This style of playing is known as *"legato"* and requires that the notes within the slur be played without breaks or pauses.

CADENCES

Musical phrases end with what is known as a "CADENCE". This describes the musical effect that occurs at the end of phrase—at the end of most pieces of music this usually means a return to the tonic chord. The most common type is the PERFECT CADENCE which describes a resolution from the dominant (V) to the tonic (I). An IMPERFECT CADENCE usually describes a movement from the tonic (I) to the dominant (V). Creating a temporary feel, the imperfect cadence rarely ends a major passage. The PLAGAL CADENCE, moves from the subdominant (IV) to the tonic (I)—think, for example, of the "Amen" sung at the end of a hymn. Finally, an INTERRUPTED CADENCE is a movement from the dominant (V) to any degree other than the tonic (I)—usually the submediant.

A good musician will interpret a slur in a subtle way that would be impossible to define in terms of note values. The term "feel" is often used to describe what occurs in this case and comes as close as any other word to describing the magical processes at work.

TIME OUT: SUMMARY OF LESSON 8

Here is a summary of the topics that we have covered in this lesson.

- Triplets and other irregular divisions
- Grouping notes
- Grouping rests
- Rules of beaming
- Recognizing phrases
- Articulation and slurs

LESSON 9

Non-Diatonic Scales

The world would be a dull place if the only scales we used were the diatonic patterns that make up the major and minor scales. Fortunately, in addition to these there are lots of different combinations that can be created from the 12 half steps that lie between the tonic and the octave. In this lesson we will examine a number of "synthetic" scales, including the minor and major pentatonics, chromatic, diminished, and augmented scales.

PENTATONIC SCALES

The pentatonic scales are perhaps the oldest of the synthetic scale types—they get their name from the fact that they are built on just five notes. Different forms of the pentatonic scales have been found in ancient cultures as diverse as those of North America, Asia, and the Far East. We will be examining the two most common forms of this scale type: the minor and major pentatonics.

THE MINOR PENTATONIC SCALE

Just about every major rock musician has played a solo built on the minor pentatonic scale, often borrowing heavily from the earlier work of jazz and blues players. In fact, so common is this scale in early blues music that

it is often referred to as the "blues" scale. Essentially a natural minor scale with the 2nd and 6th notes removed, the arrangement of the intervals is as follows: STEP PLUS HALF STEP-STEP-STEP-STEP PLUS HALF STEP-STEP. When played in the key of C, the notes used are C, E♭, F, G, and B♭. There are an additional four scales that can be created from the C minor pentatonic. Known, along with the C minor pentatonic, as the PENTATONIC MODES, these are arranged as follows: E♭-F-G-B♭-C; F-G-B♭-C-E♭; G-B♭-C-E♭-F; and B♭-C-E♭-F-B. Although all of the notes are common to the C minor pentatonic, the patterns of intervals are different in each case. You can experience the sound of each of the minor pentatonic modes by listening to the CD. ☛ 🔊 9/1

STEP PLUS HALF STEP	STEP	STEP	STEP PLUS HALF STEP	STEP

C	E♭	F	G	B♭	C
(I)	(II)	(III)	(IV)	(V)	(I)

THE MAJOR PENTATONIC

The major pentatonic scale, an essential and very common feature of country music, is created by removing the 4th and 7th notes of the diatonic major scale. The resulting set of intervals follows the pattern step–step–step plus half step–step–step plus half step. This means that in the key of C the notes used are C, D, E, G, and A (the F and B having been left out). You can hear the sound of the major pentatonic scale on your CD. 9/2

C	D	E	G	A	C
(I)	(II)	(III)	(IV)	(V)	(I)

STEP   STEP   STEP PLUS HALF STEP   STEP   STEP PLUS HALF STEP

CHROMATIC SCALE

The chromatic scale is built using every note that lies between the tonic and the octave. This means, of course, that all of the intervals are equal, each being precisely one half step.

Although music built entirely on the chromatic scale is relatively rare, use of chromatic notes is really quite common in most forms of music, usually appearing as ornamental effects or "trills." Chromatic notes can also be introduced to a piece of music in order to create a sense of tonal ambiguity. Taken to its logical conclusion, the chromatic scale can also be used to create atonal music, which as the name implies has no tonal center or tonic.

The journey towards atonal music began in the late sixteenth century, when chromatic "passing" notes were first used, adding color to the music without affecting the general tonality.

During the late nineteenth century, there was a marked increase in the use of chromaticism in serious composition and, inevitably, by the early twentieth century composers began to break out of the bonds of tonal music. Entirely new compositional forms developed, the most notable being the 12-tone system. Leading this movement was the German composer Arnold Schoenberg, who is quite rightly credited as the "father" of serial music. This music abandoned the notion of a tonal center in favour of an approach that placed equal emphasis on all 12 notes of the chromatic scale.

The staff below shows a one-octave chromatic scale laid out between two "C" notes, although the arrangement of intervals would be identical regardless of which note comes first. 9/3

THE DIMINISHED SCALE

The regular diminished scale is created using alternating intervals of a step followed by a half step. Because the arrangement of intervals is consistent, it is possible to start the diminished scale from any one of four different points. These are the 1st, 3rd, 5th, and 7th notes of the scale. This means that we need only three sets of notes to create diminished scales for all keys. ☞ 🔊 9/4

I	II	III	IV	V	VI	VII	VIII
C	D	E♭	F	G♭	G♯	A	B
C♯	D♯	E	F♯	G	A	B♭	C
D	E	F	G	A♭	B♭	B	C♯

☞ 🔊 9/4

AN ALTERNATIVE DIMINISHED SCALE

An alternative diminished scale can be created by reversing the pattern of the regular diminished scale. Simply start with a half step followed by a step and then repeat the pattern. If you look at the table of key centers on the left you will notice that alternative diminished scales can be built on the 2nd, 4th, and 6th notes of the scale. Only three sets of notes are needed to create alternative diminished scales in every key.

	STEP	HALF STEP	STEP	HALF STEP	STEP	HALF STEP	STEP	HALF STEP

C	D	E♭	F	G♭	G♯	A	B	C
(I)	(II)	(III)	(IV)	(V)	(VI)	(VII)	(VIII)	(I)

ETHNIC SCALES

The music of cultures as diverse as eastern europe, central and southeast Asia, and the Far East can be recreated, to a certain extent, by using westernized versions of the scales that are common to these parts of the world. When played in their original form, these scales can sound truly alien to our ears, especially as many of them have grown out of musical traditions that have not embraced chromatic tuning (which is typified by an octave divided equally into 12 parts). Inevitably, in adapting these scales for use in the West, certain compromises have been made, yet the scales still retain a distinct flavor of the cultures from which they are drawn.

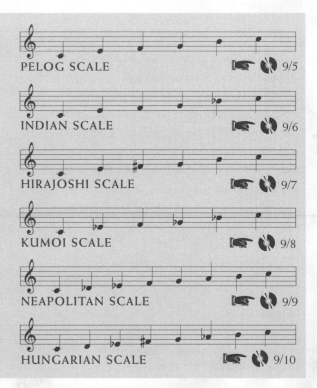

PELOG SCALE ☞ 🔊 9/5

INDIAN SCALE ☞ 🔊 9/6

HIRAJOSHI SCALE ☞ 🔊 9/7

KUMOI SCALE ☞ 🔊 9/8

NEAPOLITAN SCALE ☞ 🔊 9/9

HUNGARIAN SCALE ☞ 🔊 9/10

THE WHOLE-TONE SCALE

The augmented scale moves from the the root to the octave in just six steps, or tones. (This scale is also known as the whole-tone scale.) Obviously, this means that the pattern of intervals that makes up the scale is constructed thus: STEP-STEP-STEP-STEP-STEP-STEP.

Like the chromatic scale, the augmented scale was in use long before the twentieth century, but only came into its own as that century unfolded. Composers such as Debussy created works of breath-taking beauty using this scale, but it was perhaps Olivier Messiaen who went on to use it to greatest effect. With all of the intervals of the augmented scale being equal, it is possible to start the scale at any point and achieve the same sound. In fact, there are only really two combinations of notes needed to play the augmented scale in any key. The scale below starts on a C; the other combination would begin one half step up, on C#. Because there is no tonal center in the conventional sense, the notes of an augmented scale can be named according to personal preference.

☞ 🎧 9/11

| C | D | E | F♯ | G♯ | A♯ | C |
| (I) | (II) | (III) | (IV) | (V) | (VI) | (I) |

TEST 28

By now you should be familiar with the nine most commonly used scales in Western music: major; natural minor; harmonic minor; melodic minor; major pentatonic; minor pentatonic; chromatic; diminished; and augmented. Listen to the eight scales being played in this test and see if you can name each one.

1. ☞ 🎧 9/12   2. ☞ 🎧 9/13

3. ☞ 🎧 9/14   4. ☞ 🎧 9/15

5. ☞ 🎧 9/16   6. ☞ 🎧 9/17

7. ☞ 🎧 9/18   8. ☞ 🎧 9/19

TIME OUT: SUMMARY OF LESSON 9

The purpose of this lesson was to introduce you to the following scales:

- The major pentatonic scale
- The minor pentatonic scale
- The chromatic scale
- The diminished scales
- Ethnic scales
- The whole-tone or augmented scale

LESSON 10

Interpretation

Music might be said to comprise a combination of pitches and rhythms, but while this statement is certainly true it takes no account of the power of interpretation. The subtle effects that a good player brings to a piece of music can make all the difference between moving an audience and boring them. In this chapter we are going to look at expression marks and their effects.

DYNAMICS

When speaking, and especially when telling a good story, we tend to place emphasis on those things we consider important, using slight changes in tempo and stress to make our points (and perhaps make them funnier or more interesting). In essence, we use dynamics to make our story more appealing.

The same thing goes on in music, where dynamic effects can be used to bring out the beauty or splendor of a piece of music.

EMPHASIS

Back on page 46 we looked at how individual notes could be stressed to produce rhythmic effects within a bar full of quarter notes. We used an accent mark to indicate where these stresses should be. This was an instruction to play the note louder and was indicated by positioning the symbol "Λ" above the note or "V" below the note. Another accent mark that you are likely to come across is the symbol ">," which can be

placed either above or below the note. There is a popular perception that the symbol ">" has a milder effect than "Λ" or "V." For the most part, however, these symbols may be thought of as interchangeable.

In truth, most dynamic effects are at best rather vague instructions that are open to a wide range of interpretations. Unlike their electronic counterparts, there are no volume controls fitted to standard acoustic musical instruments (they're simply not needed). Because of this you should view accent marks as little more than an instruction to play a little louder or a little softer. For the most part the interpretation of accents will depend on the musical context—the way in which they are interpreted is largely a matter of the quality and experience of the performer. The best guide is to imagine them as herbs and spices to be used sparingly, but tastefully.

In the example below accents have been placed on every other chord in the sequence. You can hear it with and without accents on the CD.

☞ 🔊 10/1

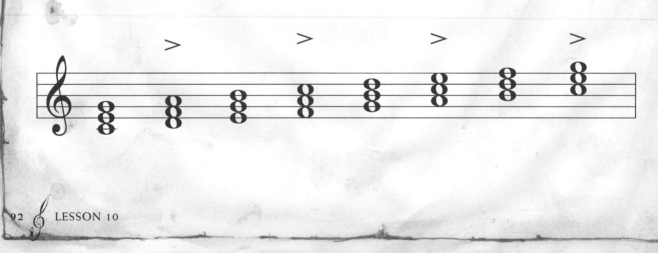

PIANO AND FORTE

We saw on page 49 that tempo can be indicated with a word or two. The same can also be said for volume. As usual, the words we use tend to be old Italian and in this case are *piano*, meaning "soft," and *forte*, meaning "loud." The two words come together to form *pianoforte*, which is the rather grand (and correct) name for the piano.

On a score these descriptions are usually abbreviated in a stylized script and positioned above or between the staves. The symbol used to show *piano* is *p*; the symbol used to show *forte* is *f*. These two letters can be further grouped together in a number of ways. An instruction to play louder than *forte* is *fortissimo*, shown as *ff*. Louder still and the composer will use the *fortississimo* symbol (*fff*). Additional *forte*

symbols can be added—some composers have used as many as six—although these are quite rare. If you look in the panel below you will see that the same process can be applied to the *piano* instruction.

Because there are no real quantifiable ways of interpreting the volume marks, once again we must use the context as our guide. The mood of a piece of music is often a good indication as to the composer's intentions.

On the staves below is an extract from a Beethoven piano sonata. If you look at the fourth bar you will see a forte symbol (*f*). This carries through to the seventh bar, when a piano symbol (*p*) appears, instructing us to quieten things down. Generally speaking, volume marks act a little like accidentals, remaining in place and in force until replaced by another mark.

INTERPRETATION MARKS

Here is a list of some of the most commonly used interpretation marks in written music.

ITALIAN NAME	DESCRIPTION	ABBREVIATION
FORTE	LOUD	*f*
PIANO	SOFT	*p*
MEZZO-FORTE	MEDIUM LOUD	*mf*
MEZZO-PIANO	MEDIUM SOFT	*mp*
FORTISSIMO	VERY LOUD	*ff*
FORTISSISSIMO	EXTREMELY LOUD	*fff*
PIANISSIMO	VERY SOFT	*pp*
PIANISSISSIMO	EXTREMELY SOFT	*ppp*
FORTE PIANO	LOUD THEN IMMEDIATELY SOFT	*fp*
POCO FORTE	SLIGHTLY LOUD	*pf*
SFORZATO/SFORZANDO	PLAYED WITH FORCE	*sf*
RINFORZATO/RINFORZANDO	BECOMING STRONGER	*rf*
SMORZANDO	GRADUALLY FADING	*smorz*
CALANDO	SLOWER WITH DECREASING VOLUME	*cal*

LOUDER AND SOFTER

An additional couple of marks are used when indicating changes in volume that occur gradually over the course of a few notes or even bars. The *Crescendo* and *diminuendo* (or *decrescendo*) marks are used for this purpose. *Crescendo* literally means "getting louder." *Diminuendo* translates as "getting softer." These are notated on the staff using either the two arrow symbols shown on the right or the abbreviations *cresc* and *dim*.

Where these changes occur over the course of perhaps a few bars, the arrow marks are stretched to cover the beginning of the effect up until the point where the desired effect has been reached.

In the example below a *crescendo* has been indicated that is supposed to take place over four bars. In this

CRESCENDO

DIMINUENDO

case the use of the symbols at the beginning and end of the *crescendo* indicate that during this time the volume should increase from *piano* to *fortissimo*. These additional symbols are not always used and so the interpretation will be dependent on the context and the performer.  10/2

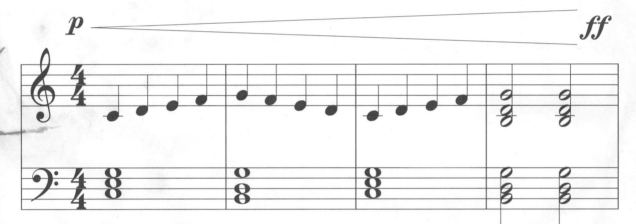

STACCATO

The term *"staccato"*, which literally means "short," is an instruction to shorten the length of a note. There are a number of ways of indicating this instruction on the staff, but the most common is to place a dot directly above the note to be shortened.

As usual, of course, the degree to which the note is shortened is open to interpretation, although it should certainly not be taken as an instruction to shorten the note as much as possible. When playing staccato passages one should try to keep the notes to a consistent length.

On the right are a number of examples of the use of the staccato symbol, applied in this case to quarter notes and to eighth notes. On the CD you can hear the first bar played both with and without the staccato effect. 10/3

STACCATO BAR

SHORTENED EQUIVALENTS

EMBELLISHMENTS

An embellishment is a symbol or instruction that is by its very nature wide open to interpretation. If anything, these symbols are used deliberately to allow the great performer to apply his or her own interpretation to the music. These embellishments take several forms and over the next couple of pages we shall be looking at what they are, what they do and how they should be approached. As ever, though, there is no set way to interpret these marks.

THE ACCIACCATURA

If you play a lot of music, then before too long you are bound to come across a note prefixed by another note printed in a much smaller script. This is called an ACCIACCATURA or an APPOGGIATURA and the note itself is sometimes referred to as a grace note.

The acciaccatura is shown with a stroke through the stem and is sometimes referred to as a crushed note. This is actually a fairly accurate indication of how the note sounds when played. The acciaccatura can be played in a number of different ways. It can be played just before the beat, on the beat but with the accent placed heavily on the main note, or at the same time as the main note but played staccato. This last method can, of course, only be used on polyphonic instruments such as guitars or pianos.

The important point to remember about grace notes is that they are never included in calculation of the length of a bar of music.

Below are two examples of the acciaccatura in use. The sixteenth notes in the second bar should be played as quickly as possible, as you will hear on the CD. 🖘 💿 10/4

THE APPOGGIATURA

Although the appoggiatura appears to be similar to the acciaccatura (but without the stroke), it does differ in one important way. The note always falls on the beat before resolving to the principal note. In other words, the appoggiatura does literally lean on the main note. (Appoggiatura means "leaning.")

The musician faces two problems when dealing with the appoggiatura. The first is that it can appear to be the same thing as an acciaccatura—an easy mistake to make. The second is that although the appoggiatura is usually shown as an eighth note it does not necessarily mean that it subtracts an eighth note from the principal note. In the eighteenth century C.P.E. Bach (son of J.S.) stated that the appoggiatura was worth half the value of the principal note if it was divisible by two, and two-thirds if it was divisible by three. Of course, interpretation of the appoggiatura should always remain at the discretion of the performer, but this rule is bound to be of help to those who are unsure of just what to make of this instruction.

On the staff below there are two appoggiature. These are being used as grace notes to the main chords, but if you look closely you will notice that the grace notes apply only to the top note in each chord. Clearly, this indicates that the grace note is not the only note to land on the beat. The grace note and the other two notes of the chord are struck simultaneously before being resolved, with the suspended 4th (F) resolving on to the 5th (G).

🖘 💿 10/5

TRILLS AND MORDENTS

A "trill" is a commonly used ornamental effect. Sometimes called a "shake," it is a note that is alternated at rapid speed with the next note above in the same key. This effect can be indicated either by placing the symbol "*tr*" above the note, or by a wavy line (some even show both). This is how you should interpret a trill placed above a quarter note.

 10/6

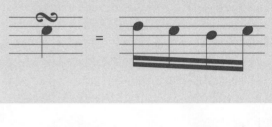

As ever, the trill is open to interpretation and it may be the case that rather than a whole series of notes one might choose instead to introduce just a single other note. This can only be determined by the context and the performer's sense of taste.

An alternative type of trill, one in which the principal note alternates with the note below (rather than above) is called a "mordent". It is shown as a wavy line with a vertical stroke (upper mordent). The inverse effect is shown as a regular wavy line (lower mordent).

TURNS

If you see a single note with the sideways "s" symbol placed above it, this is an instruction to play the note with a flourish, using the two adjacent notes. In the example shown below, a quarter-note C is played as D-C-B-C in a group of sixteenth notes. If the symbol appears between two notes then the turn is performed so as to lead into the second note.

LOWER MORDENT   UPPER MORDENT

TREMOLO

It is quite common to hear the words "vibrato" and "tremolo" used as synonyms. This is unfortunate, as they are two distinct effects.

The tremolo effect involves the fast repetition of a single note. On stringed instruments this is achieved by rapid up and down strokes, be it with the bow on a violin or the use of a plectrum on a guitar. The same effect can also be achieved on the piano.

A tremolo can be indicated using repeat strokes through the stem of the note, although this notation has other uses. 10/7

TREMOLO   ALTERNATIVE

VIBRATO

Vibrato lends a certain richness to the sound both of string instruments and the human voice. It is a slight but consistent variation in pitch which creates a much fuller sound, especially where natural reverberation causes notes to blend together, for example in an auditorium.

String players create the vibrato effect by rocking the left hand back and forth from the wrist. Wind players achieve the same effect by the careful regulation of the flow of breath. Fixed-pitch instruments such as the piano cannot perform the vibrato effect. 10/8

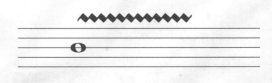

VIBRATO

REPEATING MUSIC

Over time a number of methods have evolved to indicate repetition in music. For the most part these came about as attempts to save time for the poor soul who would have written out orchestral scores.

Most forms of music rely on a degree of repetition. This helps to fix melodies and progressions in the ear of the listener, but obviously if the music has already been written out, why do it again? This is where repeat marks come into their own.

REPEATING NOTES

The use of a single stroke through any kind of note is an instruction to play the same number of eighth notes that would make up the value of that note. This is standard musical notation and so is widely used. If you examine the example on the top right, you will see that a single stroke above or below a whole note indicates that eight eighth notes are to be played in its place.

Clearly, this is a much more time-efficient way of writing out these bars. As with other forms of musical notation, the addition of extra lines can be used to indicate that more notes should be played. As you can see from the fourth, fifth, and sixth examples given,

drawing two lines through the stem of a note indicates that sixteenths should be played up to the value of that note. This gives us sixteen sixteenths in example four, eight sixteenths in example five and four sixteenths in example six. Adding an extra line to the stem would indicate that one should play twice as many notes.

REPEATING WITHIN BARS

Entire bars of music can be repeated without the need to write them out again by use of special repeat symbols. These are very commonly found on chord charts, which are an informal method for writing out harmony and are favored in particular by guitarists.

An oblique slash following a chord within a bar is an instruction to repeat that chord on as many beats of the bar as there are slashes. In the example shown below a

C major chord is repeated on each beat of the first bar. In the second bar the information is conveyed using just one chord followed by three slashes.

Notes arranged in groups within the bar can also be repeated in this way. A single slash following a group of beamed eighth notes is an instruction to repeat that group. A double stroke ("//") is used to repeat a group of sixteenth notes; a triple stroke ("///") to repeat a group of thirty-second notes.

REPEATING COMPLETE BARS

A slash symbol with dots either side (𝄎) is used when the composer wishes to repeat an entire bar of music. The symbol is placed after a bar of music and can often be repeated over several more bars.

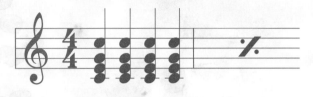

REPEATING REST BARS

If you have ever been to see an orchestra perform, you cannot fail to have noticed that not everyone is playing all of the time. In fact, percussion players in particular seem to spend most of the performance doing nothing much at all. In reality, everyone is counting, making certain that they maintain their place in the score and are ready to play when called upon. These long periods of nothing much happening are usually indicated by rests in the music and quite naturally composers came up with ways of indicating these long rest periods.

The shorthand techniques that evolved to indicate these rests include a selection of multiple-bar rest symbols that were designed for gaps of between two and eight bars. If the rest is longer than this.

SHORT REPEATS

The Italian word "bis", meaning "twice" is sometimes used as an alternative when repeating bars of music. A square bracket indicating the extent of bars affected is usually written above the music.

convention dictated that the bar appeared with a thick horizontal line and a number above it. This told the player how many bars of rest were required.

The example below shows an instruction that the player must rest for 32 bars in total.

REPEATING SECTIONS

One can easily become confused by the various, and sometimes apparently contradictory, methods used to indicate repetition. Earlier in the tutor we looked at the use of two dots and a double bar line to indicate that an entire passage was to be repeated and we need to look at that again just to be on the safe side.

Look at the example below and follow the sequence of events on the right. As you work through the example (and do take the time to do it properly), you will begin to see how a logical "order" of events is laid out with the use of repeat marks.

1. Play bars 1 and 2.
2. The repeat sign at the end of bar 2 sends you back to the start of the piece.
3. Repeat bars 1 and 2.
4. This time you ignore the repeat sign at the end of bar 2—you only react to it once, otherwise you will never get beyond bar 2.
5. Play bars 3 and 4.
6. The repeat sign at the end of bar 4 instructs you to return to the previous "start repeat" sign, which is at the beginning of bar 3.
7. Repeat bars 3 and 4, and continue onward.

BAR 1   BAR 2   BAR 3   BAR 4

OTHER REPEAT INSTRUCTIONS

Far larger and more complex repetitions can be achieved through the use of the *da capo* and *dal segno* symbols. *Da capo* means "from the head" and is an instruction to repeat the music from the start until the score indicates *fine* ("the end") or some other instruction. *Da capo* is usually shown as "D.C." beneath the final bar.

The *dal segno* symbol, which literally means "from the sign," works in a similar fashion and is an instruction that the music has to be repeated from the sign "𝄋". Once more, the music is played through until reaching *fine*.

ENDINGS

An alternative ending can be indicated by the use of first- and second-time bar brackets. In this example, bars

1 to 4 are played to the repeat sign. Bars 1 to 3 are then replayed and the first-time bar is ignored after the first cycle. Having already played it the first time around, the player now goes directly to bar 5 completing the four-bar sequence. ☜ ◑ 10/9

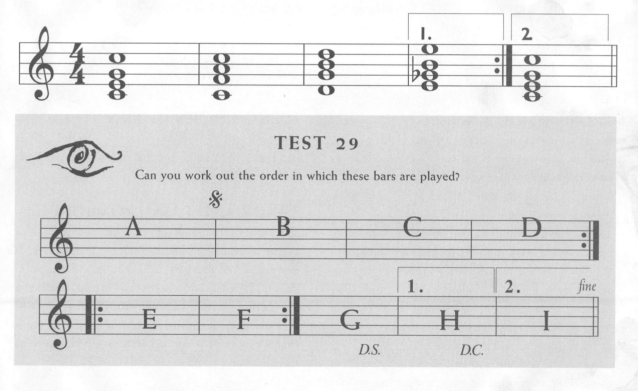

TEST 29

Can you work out the order in which these bars are played?

TIME OUT: SUMMARY OF LESSON 10

Here is a summary of the main points covered in this lesson.

- Dynamic marks
- Staccato
- Acciaccatura and appoggiatura
- Trills and mordents
- Tremolo and vibrato
- Repeat symbols

APPENDIX A

Special Cases

All instrumentalists have to learn about the notation for pitch, rhythm, and harmony. However, several instruments, especially the brass and reed instruments, are affected by other factors. Some instruments are known as transposing instruments. This means that the note written is not necessarily the one played. Over the next four pages we shall identify the special cases.

BRASS INSTRUMENTS

Brass instruments present a special problem for anyone attempting to write out notation. They belong to the family of transposing instruments, which means that the notes played are actually at a different pitch from the ones written on the paper. The trumpet (below) provides a classic example of this type of instrument.

TRUMPET (DOWN TO B♭)

When a trumpet player reads and plays the note C, what the listener hears is the note of B♭ in relation to concert pitch. Any composer or arranger who wishes to hear a trumpet play notes in the key of C must write the music out in the key of D.

This might sound like a very tiresome thing to do, but in reality it's a fairly straightforward operation. Whatever interval the instrument transposes by, one must simply adjust in the opposite direction. For example, because the trumpet transposes down by a major second (C to B♭), the music has to be transcribed up by the same amount, from C to D.

Across the page you will see the ranges for a variety of different instruments. In each case the top note is the one that is read by the musician while the bottom note reflects the true concert pitch.

PICCOLO TRUMPET (UP TO D)

This particularly high-pitched trumpet transposes up by a major second to D, which is why it is also known as the "D trumpet." Its range is identical to the conventional trumpet, but its sound is very different, especially in the higher register.

CORNET (DOWN TO B♭)

The cornet is essentially a trumpet but with conical, rather than cylindrical tubing.

FLUGELHORN (DOWN TO B♭)

The flugelhorn obeys the same rules as the trumpet, though with a slightly limited range.

FRENCH HORN (DOWN TO F)

The French horn transposes down by a perfect 5th. It has a very wide range and can be notated over both bass and treble clefs.

TENOR AND BASS TROMBONE

The tenor trombone is the correct name for the instrument most of us know as a trombone. It is notated on the bass clef. The first three notes shown are pedal tones, or drones—the notes between the highest pedal (B♭) and the bottom end of the playable range (E) are not possible on a trombone. Both tenor and bass trombones play at concert pitch.

TUBA

Music for the tuba is written in the bass clef because it is the lowest-pitched brass instrument. The notes below the lowest "F" can only be played as pedal tones. A small number "8" below the bottom note is used to indicate that it is actually an octave lower than the notes defined by the bass clef.

There are a number of different types of tuba, but they generally play at concert pitch.

TRUMPET (E-B♭)   FLUGELHORN (E-A♭)

FRENCH HORN (B-F)

BASS TROMBONE (E-B♭)   TROMBONE (A♭-B♭)   TUBA (C-F)

WIND INSTRUMENTS

Several members of the wind family, just like their brass counterparts, are transposing instruments.

ALTO FLUTE (DOWN TO G)

The alto flute transposes down by a perfect 4th. The bass flute transposes down by an octave. The regular "concert" flute, however, plays at concert pitch.

BASSOON

The bassoon is as a "double reed" instrument. It does not have a conventional mouthpiece, Instead, it has two reeds tied together. Its treble equivalent, the oboe, also plays at concert pitch.

CLARINET (DOWN TO B♭)

The B♭ clarinet is the most common variety but there are several different types.

SAXOPHONE FAMILY (VARIOUS)

All saxophones are transposing instruments, although they have very different pitch ranges. The complete range is as follows: the soprano saxophone transposes down to B♭; the alto, down to E♭; the tenor down to B♭ beyond the octave; and the baritone down to E♭ beyond the octave.

ALTO FLUTE (G-G)

CLARINET (G-F)

OBOE (B♭-G)

BASSOON (B♭-E♭)

SAXOPHONES
SOPRANO (A♭-E♭)
ALTO (D♭-D♭)
TENOR (A♭-E♭)
BARITONE (D♭-D♭)

THE STRING FAMILY

The four instruments that make up the string family are the violin, viola, cello, and double bass, but the double bass is the only transposing instrument among them. The way each instrument is tuned is shown in brackets, with strings named from the lowest to the highest.

VIOLIN (G – D – A – E)

The violin has a practical range of G below middle C to the note E three-and-a-half octaves higher. It is the highest-pitched instrument in the string family.

VIOLA (C – G – D – A)

The viola is similar in appearance to the violin, if a little larger, and is lower in pitch. Some of the written music for the viola is placed on the alto clef because of the range of the instrument. The notes on the alto clef are F-A-C-E-G (lines) and G-B-D-F (spaces).

CELLO (VIOLONCELLO) (C – G – D – A)

While music for the cello is sometimes written on the tenor clef, in practice most cellists are more familiar with the bass clef.

DOUBLE BASS (E – A – D – G)

Parts written for the double bass are transposed up by an octave and so its pitch range of E to G is written an

VIOLIN (G-E)

VIOLA (C-A)

CELLO (C-E)   DOUBLE BASS (E-G)

octave higher. By raising the music on to the staff, it becomes easier to read, not least because failing to do this would result in most of the notes appearing on ledger lines. Music written for the acoustic or electric bass guitar is treated in the same way.

Although notes higher than G are possible, even among good players intonation can suffer in this register. More likely than not, the arranger would move the part over to a cello before reaching this range.

THE VOICE

For the last two hundred years or so, singing voices have been classified according to two pairs of basic types: BASS and TENOR for males; ALTO and SOPRANO for females. The approximate pitch ranges for these categories are shown below. There is considerable crossover between each pair and most normal singing voices tend to fit somewhere between each range. This means that most male voices are BARITONE while most female voices can be classified as MEZZO-SOPRANO. BASSO-PROFUNDO is an exceptionally low male bass voice. A male alto voice is called a COUNTER TENOR (or just plain "annoying"), while a falsetto voice is a MALE SOPRANO.

BASS   TENOR

ALTO   SOPRANO

DRUMS AND PERCUSSION

Music for drums and the rest of the percussion family varies depending on precisely which instrument is being written for. Instruments like the glockenspiel and xylophone use standard notation, written respectively one and two octaves lower, because they are capable of producing melodic lines. Pitched percussion, such as the timpani (kettle drum), has a limited range which can be captured on the bass clef. Glissandos are used to indicate any changes in pitch produced by a foot pedal or tuning key.

The drum kit is a fairly modern arrangement of instruments (individual drums and cymbals) and as such has almost no role in the regular classical repertoire. In the popular music idioms most composers and arrangers leave the drum parts to the discretion of the drummers, although some will provide perhaps general instructions relating to style and feel. Even among jazz musicians it is still rare for a full drum kit part to be notated and most arrangers usually ask merely for a particular style ("Shuffle," "Swing," etc.).

It is possible to provide notation for a full drum kit using a staff with a time signature, but no clef. The lines and spaces are used to score different drum voices, with standard notation providing the note values. As you can see in the example below, the hi-hats are playing in eighths, the snare drum crashes in on beats two and four, while the bass drum mostly plays on each beat of the bar.

GUITAR (E – A – D – G – B – E)

To be technically correct, guitar music should be shown on a treble clef with a small "8" on its tail—this denotes that all the music written on this staff should be played an octave higher. (This means that the guitar is a transposing instrument.) In practice, this convention is rarely observed

In the notation on the right you will notice that the guitar appears to have a four-octave range. In reality, this can only be achieved by certain types of electric guitar (mostly those with 24 frets) and for the most part the upper register of the classical guitar tends to be avoided, not least because it is actually physically difficult to reach notes in the upper register. Sometimes a composer may try to get around this problem by using harmonics (see Appendix B, page 110), which can be played on lower frets but sound much higher.

It is also possible to play notes below the standard range of the instrument by re-tuning it. This is a deviation from the standard tuning (shown above right) but can be used to very dramatic effect, bringing out a richness in the bass notes that is sometimes lacking in many classical guitars. The descent into the lower register is limited, however, by the amount the bottom string or strings can be lowered. Anything beyond a major 3rd down tends to cause the string to become too slack to be played, even on instruments fitted with an extra bass string for this very purpose.

PIANO

The piano, from the smallest of "uprights" to the largest of concert grands, comes in a wide variety of shapes and sizes. The concert grand piano has one of the widest pitch ranges of any instrument, beginning with the note A over three octaves below middle C up to the note C, three octaves above middle C. Octave symbols are added above the treble staff and below the bass staff to notate music across this massive range.

Dictionary of Special Musical Terms

There are far too many standard musical terms for us to cover in the relatively limited space we have here; we could easily fill another book and still not have covered them all. What we can offer, however, is a list of the essential terms (and a few fun ones for good measure) in the hope that this will cover you for most eventualities. Should you need reminding, this list also covers all the terms used throughout the tutor.

ABSTOSSEN
See Staccato.

A CAPPELLA
Choral music sung without the accompaniment of a musical instrument.

ACCELERANDO
Becoming faster.

ACCENT
An emphasis that is placed on specific notes of chords within a sequence, making them louder or creating rhythmic effects.

ACCIACCATURA
An ornamental effect sometimes called a "crushed note." The acciaccatura acts as a prefixes to a regular note and is shown in small type to indicate that its duration does not contribute to the overall value of the bar. The two notes should be struck so that the acciaccatura is barely perceptible, appearing on the beat of the principal note.

ACCOLADE
See Brace.

ACCIDENTAL
Symbols used in written music to raise or lower the pitch of a note by one or two half steps. A sharp (♯) raises the pitch by a half step; a double sharp (✗) raises the pitch by two half steps; a flat (♭) lowers the pitch by a half step; and the double flat (♭♭) lowers the pitch by two half steps. The effect of sharps and flats can be cancelled with the use of a symbol known as a natural sign and indicated thus: ♮.

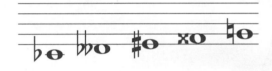

ACCOMPANIMENT
Any form of musical backing. Although this usually applies to vocalists, it can also be used to distinguish between primary and secondary musical roles.

ACCORDARE/ACCORDER
To tune.

ACOUSTIC(S)
A non-electric instrument; the science of the behavior of sound.

ACTION
The mechanism on a piano or organ that creates a sound when a key is played; the height of the strings above the frets on a guitar.

ADAGIO
A slow tempo which is faster than *andante* but slower than *largo*. Literally meaning "at ease," its diminutive form is *adagietto*, which is slightly faster than *adagio*.

ADAGISSIMO
Slower than *adagio*—extremely slow.

ADDED NINTH CHORD

An interval of a 9th added above the root of a triad. This differs from a 9th chord, where a 9th is simply added to a 7th chord.

ADDOLORATO

Performance mark whose literal meaning is "pained" or "stricken."

AD LIBITUM

Instruction that the performer may freely interpret or improvise a passage. It may also mean that within a score a vocal or instrumental part may be omitted.

AOLIAN MODE

Modal scale starting on the sixth degree of the major scale.

AFFETUOSO

Direction that a piece should be performed tenderly; a term loosely connected to the seventeenth-century Doctrine of Affections, a belief held by a group of composers that the function of music should be to arouse the passions of the listener, be it with love, hate or joy.

AGITATO

Performance direction meaning "agitated."

AIR

A tune—vocal or instrumental.

ALBERTI BASS

A bass figure made popular by the Italian composer Domenico Alberti (1710–1740) in which the notes of a triad were played in a first-fifth-third-fifth sequence. The most significant example is Mozart's "PIANO SONATA in C major (K.545)."

ALLA BREVE

Played with a half-note beat—equates to a time signature of two-two.

ALLA MARCIA

To be played in the style of a march.

ALLEGRO

Literally meaning "quickly," this indicates that the music should be played at a fast tempo. Its diminutive form is *allegretto*, which is fast, but not as fast as *allegro*.

ALTERED CHORD

A chord in which one or more of the pitches has been altered by the addition of an accidental.

ALTO

A low female voice or a high male voice; the second highest vocal range, beneath soprano and above tenor.

ANDANTE

Medium-speed tempo played "at walking pace." *Andantino* usually means slightly faster than *andante*. *Molto andante* indicates that the tempo should be set slower than *andante*.

ANIMANDO

Literally meaning "becoming animated"—an increase in tempo is also implied. Note, however, the related term *anima* has a slightly ambiguous meaning which can be interpreted as an instruction to play with feeling or with spirit.

APPOGGIATURA

Distinct from the accacciatura, this is a grace note or "leaning" note which receives half the value of the principal note. It can also be used to indicate pitch bends on stringed instruments.

WRITTEN   PLAYED

ARCHETTO/ARCO

The bow of a stringed instrument.

ARCHO/ARCHI

An instruction to resume playing with the bow after having played *pizzicato*.

ARIA

A self-contained piece of music for a single voice with instrumental accompaniment. The aria commonly forms a part of a larger work, such as an opera.

ARPEGGIO

The notes of a chord played in quick succession (rather than simultaneously) from lowest notes to highest and commonly notated using a wavy line.

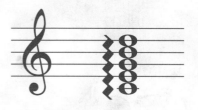

ARTICULATION

The attack with which single notes or chords are played and the length of time over which they are allowed to decay. Articulation symbols written on the staff can include the slur, which marks out phrases, and staccato, which shortens the length of a note.

A TEMPO

An instruction to return to the original tempo after deviations. Literally meaning "in time."

ATONAL

Music composed with the deliberate suppression of the central tonic triad or use of diatonic harmony, allowing the 12 pitches of the chromatic scale to be used freely.

AUGMENTED

Interval created by raising a perfect or major interval by a half step.

AUXILIARY NOTE

Used in counterpoint to describe a note which is a step above or below a consonant note.

BACKBEAT

Term used in modern music to describe the rhythmic effect of a heavy snare drum beat on the second and fourth beats of a bar.

BAR

A unit of musical time. The notes contained within a bar total a fixed combined value defined by the time signature. Sometimes referred to as a "measure," bars are separated by bar lines.

BARRE

Method of playing polyphonic stringed instruments such as the guitar by positioning the index finger across the strings enabling the player to hold down adjacent notes of a chord along the fingerboard.

BASS

The lowest part in a polyphonic composition; the lowest-pitched male voice; term used to describe the double bass or the bass guitar; a range of low frequencies that can be electronically filtered.

BEAT

A metrical pulse grouped together to form recurring patterns or rhythms.

BEL CANTO

A singing technique which emphasizes an even tone throughout the vocal range—literally means "beautiful singing."

BIND

See Tie.

BIS

An instruction to repeat a short passage.

BITONALITY

The simultaneous use of two or more keys within a piece of music.

BRACE

Symbol used to join together staves that are to be played simultaneously. Piano music usually shows a treble staff and a bass staff played by the right and left hands respectively.

BRASS INSTRUMENTS

A family of tubular wind instruments which includes the trumpet, tuba, and trombone.

BRAVURA, CON

An instruction that a composition or passage requires a virtuoso display by the performer.

BREATH MARKS

Symbol used in vocal music to denote where breath should be taken. Usually shown as "✱."

BREVE/BREVIS

The short note in mensural notation (the counterpart to the *longa*—long note) the modern-day equivalent of two half notes.

BROKEN CHORD

See Arpeggio.

CADENCE

A musical phrase that creates the sense of rest or resolution at its end. The most commonly used cadence is the "perfect cadence" (V-I).

CADENZA

An ornamental passage frequently performed over the penultimate notes or chord in a cadence. In most cases this cadence signals the end of the composition or movement and will resolve to the tonic.

CADENZATO

Rhythmic.

CALANDO

Getting softer—dying away.

CALMATO

Play in a calm, tranquil manner.

CANTARE SUPER LIBRUM

Vocal improvisation on an existing melody.

CAPO/CAPOTASTO

Mechanical bar fitted to a fretted stringed instrument for the purposes of transposition.

CAPRICCIOSO

Instruction that a piece should be played capriciously or at the player's whim.

CASTRATO

A male singer castrated as a child in order to preserve his alto or soprano vocal range. Also known as "eviratos," castratos were widely used in operatic music during the seventeenth and eighteenth centuries.

CELERE/CELEREMENTE

Instruction to play swiftly.

CHAMBER MUSIC

Compositions created to be performed for a small ensemble, most notably a string quartet.

CHANSON

The French word for "song." The term has a wide variety of ambiguous uses in music.

CHORAL MUSIC

Music performed by a choir or chorus with each individual part sung by more than one vocalist.

CHORD

The sound of three or more notes of different pitch played simultaneously. A three-note chord is known as a "triad."

CHROMATIC

A scale that includes all 12 pitches, with each degree separated by a half step.

CIRCLE OF FIFTHS

Closed circle of all 12 pitches arranged at intervals of a perfect 5th and first devised by Johann David Heinichen in the eighteenth century.

CLEF

Symbol placed at the beginning of a staff or bar line that determines the pitches of the notes and lines on the staff that follow. Three types are commonly used: the G or treble clef; the F or bass clef; and the C clef. The C clef as shown is termed the alto clef and when centered on the fourth line it becomes the tenor clef.

TREBLE   BASS   ALTO

CLOSE HARMONY

Term to describe the three uppermost voices singing in close triads in four-part harmony,

CODA

The concluding passage of a piece of music.

COMMON CHORD

A major triad.

COMMON TIME

Music written with a time signature of four-four or two-two. Indicated by the clef symbols "**C**" (four-four) and "**₵**" (two-two).

COMODO

Instruction to play at a comfortable speed.

COMPOUND INTERVAL

An interval of greater than an octave.

CONCERT PITCH

The set of reference tones to which all non-transposing instruments must be tuned. Commonly the note "A" below "middle C" and measured as having a frequency of 440 cycles/second.

CONCORD

The description given to intervals that are deemed to be consonant. Specifically, they are the intervals between the root note (first) and the third, fourth, fifth, sixth, and eighth notes respectively.

CONTRALTO

The lowest female voice.

COUNTERMELODY

A subordinate melody that accompanies a main melody.

COUNTERPOINT

Two or more lines of melody played at the same time.

COUNTER TENOR

A male alto.

CRESCENDO

A performance mark that indicates a gradual increase in loudness. The opposite of *diminuendo* or *decrescendo*.

CROTCHET

A note worth one beat within a bar of four-four time.

DA CAPO

Literally meaning "from the head," *da capo* is an instruction that the performer must return to the beginning of the piece and conclude at the double bar marked *fine*, or an alternative repeat sign such as *dal segno* or "𝄋." The term is usually abbreviated as *D.C.*

DAL SEGNO

Literally meaning "from the sign," an instruction that the performer must repeat a sequence from a point marked by the sign "𝄋." Abbreviated as *D.S.*

DAMP

Muting with the right hand or the immediate loosening of the fingers of the left hand in order to stop the vibration of a string or strings.

DECISO/DECISAMENTE

Instruction to play decisively with resolve.

DECRESCENDO

See Crescendo and Diminuendo.

DELICATO

Instruction to play delicately.

DEMISEMIQUAVER

A thirty-second note—a note whose value is an eighth of a beat within a four-four bar. See Notes.

DIABOLUS IN MUSICA

The "devil in music"; the name given in the seventeenth century to the "tritone"—an interval of three whole steps. Deemed dissonant, the use of the interval was prohibited by various music theorists of the time.

DIATONIC

The seven-note major and minor scale system.

DIMINISHED

An interval created by lowering a perfect or minor interval by a half step; also a term applied both to a minor chord with a lowered fifth note and a chord that comprises minor 3rd intervals.

DIMINUENDO

A performance mark that indicates a gradual decrease in loudness. The opposite of *crescendo*. Sometimes referred to as *decrescendo*.

DISCORD

Note intervals that are deemed to be dissonant in character. Specifically this refers to the intervals between the root note (first) and the second and seventh notes respectively.

DOMINANT

The fifth degree of a major or minor scale. The triad built on this degree is the dominant triad; the 7th built on this degree is the dominant 7th.

DOPPIO MOVIMENTO
An instruction to perform a passage at double the tempo.

DORIAN MODE
The modal scale built from the second degree of the major scale.

DOTTED NOTES
A dot positioned after any type of note and which increases its value by half. A second dot can be added to increase the value by a quarter; a third dot added increases the value by an eighth.

DOTTED RESTS
A dot positioned after a rest to increase its value by half. Most commonly found in compound time.

DOUBLE
To perform the same set of notes on two instruments. The two parts can be played at the same pitch or an interval of an octave.

DOUBLE BAR
Two vertical lines drawn through the staff to indicate the end of a piece of music or a movement.

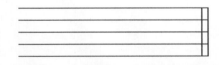

DOUBLE FLAT
See Accidentals.

DOUBLE SHARP
See Accidentals.

DUET
A composition for two performers.

DUOLO/DOLORE
Instruction to play with sorrow or grief.

DYNAMIC MARKS
Terms, symbols, and abbreviations used to indicate different levels of volume or a transition from one level to another.

EMBOUCHURE
The correct positioning of the lips and mouth for players of wind instruments.

EMPFINDUNG, MIT
German-language term—an instruction to perform with feeling or emotion.

ENHARMONIC
A set of different names that may be applied to the same pitches. For example, the notes D♯ and E♭ are deemed to be enharmonic equivalents.

ESPRESSIVO
Instruction to play expressively.

EXPRESSION MARKS
Words or symbols written on a score to guide the player on matters other than pitch or rhythm—dynamics, articulation, and tempo, for example.

FACILE/FACILMENTE
Play easily.

FALSETTO
A male voice that sings in the female soprano range.

FERMATA
Pause. A symbol placed above or below a note or rest that indicates that it should be held for longer than its natural duration. Before the twentieth century it was traditionally known as a "corona."

FLAT
See Accidentals.

FLEBILE
Plaintive or mournful.

FORTE/FORTISSIMO/FORTISSISSIMO
A set of instructions for the performer to play louder, of which *forte* is the quietest and *fortissimo* the loudest. The terms are abbreviated using a stylized script as *f*, *ff*, and *fff* respectively.

FORTE-PIANO

An instruction to play loud then soft. Shown in a stylized script as *f p*.

FORZA/FORZANDO

Instructions to play with strength or force.

FRET

A strip of metal placed across the fingerboard of some stringed instruments, such as the guitar, lute or mandolin, that fixes the pitch of the strings at a predetermined level.

FUGUE

Form of composition in which a theme, established by one voice is taken up by another. The initial voice is then used to provide a counterpoint accompaniment. This process continues irrespective of the number of voices used.

GATHERING NOTE

A reference tone provided by an organist to a choir prior to the singing of hymns.

GENERAL PAUSE

German word that literally means "general pause." A rest for all players within an orchestral score. Usually shown on the staff as "G.P."

GLISSANDO

A continuous sliding movement between two different pitches. On a piano keyboard the effect can be produced by running the nails of a finger along the black or white notes, creating a very fast scale of discretely pitched notes. On other instruments this effect creates a continuous change in pitch which is sometimes referred to as "portamento." The effect is shown on written music by joining the upper and lower notes with a line. A lower-case letter "s" may also be shown above the line.

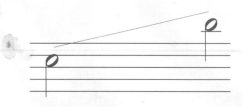

GRACE NOTE

See Appoggiatura.

GRAZIOSO

Instruction to play with grace.

GREGORIAN CHANT

Also known as plainsong, the predominant liturgical chant used during the Middle Ages.

HALF STEP

The interval between two adjacent notes.

HARMONIC

A bell-like effect created on stringed instruments by the positioning of the finger over specific points along the length of the string. Indicated by a small open circle above the note or with a diamond-headed note.

HARMONY

The effect of a set of notes played simultaneously, and how these intervals and chords sound in relation to each other.

HEMIDEMISEMIQUAVER

British term for a sixty-fourth note—worth a sixteenth of a beat within a bar of four-four. See Notes.

HEXACHORD

A simultaneous collection of six pitches.

IMPERFECT CADENCE

A cadence which moves from the tonic to the dominant—usually a phrase in the middle of a piece of music.

IMPROVISATION

At one extreme, the creation of an original work during the course of a performance. In the classical tradition improvisation tends to be limited to allowing the performer a greater degree of flexibility in ornamentation and other discretionary areas.

INTERRUPTED CADENCE

A cadence which moves from the dominant to any chord other than the tonic.

INTERVAL

The relationship between two different pitches numbered in terms of the degrees of the diatonic scale system.

INTONATION

The degree to which tuning and pitching is accurate among the musicians in an ensemble.

INVERSION

The order of notes in a chord from the lowest pitch. If the root is the lowest note, the chord is said to be in the root position. If the third note is the lowest, the chord is a first inversion; if the fifth note is the lowest, it is a second inversion; if a seventh note has the lowest pitch, the chord is called a third inversion.

IONIAN MODE

A modal scale from which the diatonic major scale was originally derived.

JOYEUX

Instruction that a piece of music should be played joyfully.

KEY

The reference pitch for a diatonic scale.

KEYNOTE

An alternative name for the first degree of a diatonic scale.

KEY SIGNATURE

An arrangement of sharps and flats on the staff that defines the key.

LAMENTOSO/LAMENTABILE

An instruction for the performer to play a piece of music with a mood of sadness.

LARGO

Slow or stately.

LONGA

In mensural notation, the long or *maxima* note.

LEADING NOTE

The seventh degree of the diatonic major scale.

LEDGER LINE

A short line that allows notes to be transcribed outside of the range of the five-line staff.

LEGATO

An instruction to play a sequence of notes as smoothly as possible with no separation between successive notes. Often indicated within the boundaries of a slur but also sometimes abbreviated as *leg*.

LEGNO

Instruction to bowed string players to strike the strings with the wood of the bow rather than the hair.

LENTO

Instruction to play extremely slowly.

L.H.

Left hand.

LIBRETTO

The text for an opera.

LICENZA

Played freely with regard to tempo or rhythm.

LIGADO

On stringed instruments such as the guitar, the effect of bringing one of the fretting fingers down on to a vibrating string to create a note of a higher pitch. The opposite principle can also be used by bringing the finger away from the vibrating string to play a note of lower pitch. These terms are commonly known as "hammering-on" and "pulling off."

LOCO

Instruction to return to original pitch having having been instructed to play at an alternative pitch, usually an interval of an octave. Abbreviated as *"loc."*

LOCRIAN MODE

Modal scale which starts on the seventh degree of the major scale.

LUGUBRE

To play mournfully.

LUNGA

Prolonged pause or period of rest.

LYDIAN MODE

Mode starting on the fourth degree of the major scale.

MAESTOSO

To play majestically.

MANCANDO

Instruction that the music should create the illusion of fading away. Abbreviated as *"manc."*

MARZIALE

Instruction to play in a military style.

M.D.
Mano destra, Main droit—right hand.

MEASURE
Alternative name for a bar.

MEDIANT
The third degree of the major scale.

MELODY
A pattern of single notes that forms a coherent sequence. Often simply described as a tune.

MENSURAL NOTATION
System of musical notation used between the thirteenth and sixteenth centuries, generally credited to Franco of Cologne (fl. ca. 1250). The principal note values were the *maxima, longa, brevis,* and *semibrevis* (shown from left to right).

METER
See Tempo.

METRONOME
Mechanical device used to denote the tempo of a piece of music in beats per minute. Often known as "Maelzel's Metronome" after the man who patented the idea. The letters "M.M." followed by a note-type and value are often used on printed music to specify the tempo.

$$\text{M.M.} \quad \clubsuit = 120$$

M.G.
Main gauche—left hand.

MICROTONE
A measurable interval smaller than a half step. Its use in Western musical forms is largely esoteric.

MIDDLE C
The center note on a piano keyboard, also an important reference tone for other orchestral instruments. It is notated on a ledger line below a staff anchored by a treble clef.

MIXOLYDIAN MODE
The mode starting on the fifth degree of the major scale.

MODE
A series of fixed scales that were predominant during the Middle Ages. The modern-day diatonic system of major and minor scales evolved from their existence. The seven modes that can be built from the major scale are Ionian (I), Dorian (II), Phrygian (III), Lydian (IV), Mixolydian (V), Aeolian (VI), and Locrian (VII).

MODERATO
Instruction to play at a moderate speed.

MODULATION
Movement from one key to another within a section or piece of music.

MONODY
Music consisting of a single melodic line.

MONOPHONY
Music that comprises a single line.

MORDENT
An ornamental instruction to play a single note as a "trill" with an adjacent note. An upper mordent (left) alternates with the note a half step higher; than lower mordent (right) is played with the note a half step lower.

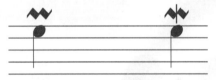

MOVEMENT
Any self-contained segment of a larger work such as a symphony or concerto.

M.S.
Mano sinistra—left hand.

MUTE
A device or technique for reducing the volume on a musical instrument. On brass instruments the mute is a conical block that when placed in the bell reduces volume and alters the tone. The equivalent effect on the piano is the use of the damper pedal.

NATURAL
See Accidentals.

NEUME

Symbols used in the notation of plainsong between the ninth and twelfth centuries.

NOTES

Symbols used in written music to indicate the pitch and duration of a sound. They are (shown from left to right): whole note, half note, quarter note, eighth note, sixteenth note, thirty-second note, and sixty-fourth note. In Europe they are usually known under an alternative naming system as: semibreve, minim, crotchet, quaver, semiquaver, demi-semiquaver, and hemidemisemiquaver.

NOUVO

New.

OBBLIGATO

Literally meaning "obligatory," a term used to describe an accompanying secondary melody which is nonetheless extremely important and should not be omitted under any circumstances.

OCTAVE

An interval whose pitches have the same note name but the frequency of the lower note is half that of the upper note. Abbreviated as "Ott," "8va," or "8ve." When these marks are written above a staff, the notes should be played an octave higher in pitch; when written below the staff they should be played an octave lower.

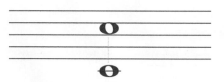

OCTET

Chamber music written for eight musicians.

ONE-LINE

Any octave interval from middle C or from the notes within the octave starting with middle C.

OPUS

A non-specific term that refers to a musical composition. It is frequently used in designating a catalogue number to a composer's work. Usually abbreviated as "op."

ORNAMENTATION

The alteration of a piece of music to make it sound more effective or beautiful, usually through the addition of notes or dynamic changes.

OSSIA

A term used to indicate an alternative version of a passage—usually one which is easier to play.

OSTINATO

A short pattern that is repeated throughout a piece of music.

OTTAVA

Italian word for octave. See Octave.

OTTAVA BASSA/OTTAVA ALTA

Octave lower/octave higher.

OVERTURE

An orchestral composition that acts as an introduction to an extended work.

PARLATO/PARLANDO

Instruction to sing in a spoken style. Most commonly used in comic opera situations.

PASSING CHORD/NOTE

A chord or note whose function is clearly subordinate to the two notes on either side. It is, in effect, a kind of harmonic intermediary.

PAUSE

See Fermata.

PEDAL TONE

A bass note that sustains beneath any shifting harmonic structure. A typical example would be the bass "drone" produced by bagpipes.

PELOG

An Indonesian tuning used in gamelan music.

PENTACHORD

A chord comprising five different pitches.

PENTATONIC

A set of scales based around five notes. Among the oldest of scalar systems, pentatonic variants are used in musical culture all over the world. The minor pentatonic "blues scale" is commonly used in jazz, R&B, and rock music.

PERDENDOSI

Performance instruction to create the effect of the music fading away.

PERFECT CADENCE

A cadence that resolves from the dominant (V) to the tonic (I). The most commonly used form of a cadence with which a piece of music is concluded.

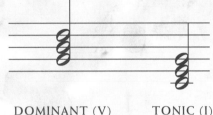

DOMINANT (V)   TONIC (I)

PERFORMANCE MARKS

Words or symbols written on a score to indicate aspects of performance not covered purely by pitches on the staff.

PHRASE

A self-contained musical sentence that can be viewed as a coherent and identifiable "whole" within the context of composition. Usually no more than a few bars in length, phrases are identified in written music within a slur.

PHRYGIAN MODE

The mode which is built from the third degree of the diatonic major scale.

PIANO/PIANISSIMO/PIANISSISSIMO

Instructions for the performer to play softer, of which *pianississimo* is the quietest. Shown in a stylized script as *p*, *pp*, and *ppp* respectively.

PIANOFORTE

The technically correct name of the piano; also a performance instruction to play loud and then soft immediately afterwards. Usually shown on the score in a stylized script as *pf*.

PIMA

The Spanish names given to the fingers of the right hand in classical guitar: "P" (*pulgar*) is the thumb; "I" (*indicio*) is the first/index finger; "M" (*medio*) is the second finger; and "A" (*anular*) is the third finger.

PITCH

The frequency of a note in terms of the number of times it vibrates each second.

PIZZICATO

In music written for strings, an instruction to pluck the notes with the fingers rather than play with a bow. Usually abbreviated as *"pizz."*

PLAGAL CADENCE

A cadence that resolves from the subdominant (IV) to the tonic (I).

SUBDOMINANT (IV)   TONIC (I)

PLECTRUM

A device usually made from plastic, horn, tortoiseshell or ivory for plucking stringed instruments such as the guitar, mandolin or banjo. The term "pick" is also used.

POCO

Literally meaning "little." Derivatives include *poco a poco* ("little by little"), *fra poco* ("shortly"), *pochetto* or *pochettino* ("very little"), and *pochissimo* ("extremely little").

POLYCHORD

A chord which is made up of two different chords.

POLYPHONY

Music that combines two or more different lines.

PORTAMENTO

See Glissando.

PRALLTRILLER

Alternative name for the upper mordent.

PRELUDE

A self-contained composition whose function is both to attract the attention of the listener and to establish the pitch, key or mood of the music that follows immediately afterwards.

PRESTO

An instruction to play very fast—faster than *allegro*.

PRIMARY TRIADS

Term describing the three triads built from the tonic, subdominant, and dominant degrees of a diatonic scale.

PRIMA/PRIMO

The Italian word that translates literally as "first"; used in conjunction with other performance marks such as *prima volta* ("first time") or *primo tempo* ("first tempo")—an instruction to revert to playing the tempo at which the composition began.

PUNTEADO

Technique by which the strings of a guitar are plucked rather than strummed.

QUARTER TONE

An interval whose value is a quarter of a step.

QUARTET

A composition written for four performers; the name given to an ensemble of four musicians.

QUAVER

British term for an eighth note. See Notes.

QUINTET

A composition written for five performers; the name given to an ensemble of five musicians.

QUINTUPLET

A group of five notes played in the time of four.

RAGA

A mode used in the music of northern India.

RASGUEADO

A method of strumming used by flamenco guitarists.

REED

A family of instruments that incorporate a reed fitted in the mouthpiece (or reeds tied together) to create their sound. The group includes the clarinet, saxophone, bassoon, and oboe. The latter two are "double-reed" instruments.

REFRAIN

A segment from within a piece of music which is repeated periodically throughout. The chorus from within a pop song is a typical example.

REGISTER

The tonal range of a voice or instrument.

RELATIVE MAJOR/RELATIVE MINOR

The relationship between major and natural minor scales: the pitch of the notes and chords built on any major scale are the same as those on a natural minor scale built from the sixth degree of the major scale.

REPEAT/REITERATE

An instruction to reiterate a piece of music within the bars specified by repeat symbols.

REPRISE

The repetition of a sequence or theme.

RESOLUTION

A movement from a dissonant note to a consonant note.

REST

A symbol placed on the staff to indicate a period in which no notes are played. Each of the different note-types has an equivalent rest. They are (from left to right): whole note, half note, quarter note, eighth note, sixteenth note, thirty-second note, and sixty-fourth note.

RESTRINGENDO

Literally meaning "becoming faster."

RETENU

Instruction to hold back and play more slowly.

R.H.

Instruction found in keyboard music to play a part with the right hand.

RHYTHM

A pattern or movement in time of notes and accents.

RIGOROSO
Strict.

RINFORZANDO
Instruction to suddenly accent notes.

RISOLUTO
Instruction to play boldly with energy.

RITARDANDO
Instruction to play gradually slower.

RITENUTO
An instruction to make a sudden reduction in tempo.

RUBATO, TEMPO
Literally meaning "stolen time." An instruction that allows the performer to ignore the prevailing tempo and speed up or slow down according to his or her own preference.

SCALE
A collection of notes laid out in a predefined sequence from the lowest pitch to the highest pitch.

C MAJOR SCALE

SCALE DEGREES
The position of each note within a scale. Can be shown numerically using Arabic or Roman numerals. Each degree can also be named: tonic (I); supertonic (II); mediant (III); subdominant (IV); dominant (V); submediant (VI); and leading note (VII).

SCHERZO/SCHERZANDO
Literally meaning "joke," an instruction to perform a piece of music playfully. There is also an implication of a fast tempo.

SCORE
The notation of an entire piece of music for an ensemble written out so that the simultaneous parts are aligned in a vertical manner.

SEGNO
Literally meaning "sign." The symbol ("𝄋") is used to mark the beginning or end of a repeated section. The sign must be paired with either a *dal segno* instruction,

which means "from the sign," or an *al segno* instruction (meaning "to the sign").

SEGUE
A term indicating that the next piece of music follows immediately with no interruption.

SEMIQUAVER
British term for a sixteenth note. See Notes.

SEMITONE
The British term for a half step—the interval between two adjacent pitches and one twelfth of an octave; the smallest interval used in most Western music.

SEMPRE
Literally meaning "always."

SEQUENCE
The repetition of a musical phrase at gradually increasing or decreasing intervals.

SEPTUPLET
A group of seven notes usually to be played in the time of four or six.

SEXTET
A composition written for six performers; the name given to an ensemble of six musicians.

SEXTUPLET
A group of six notes usually to be played in the time of four.

SFORZATO/SZFORZANDO
Literally meaning "forced" but usually interpreted as an instruction to play loud. Abbreviated as *sfz*.

SHARP
See Accidentals.

SIMILE
An instruction to continue playing as already marked; literally means "like."

SLIDE
See Glissando.

SOL-FA
A system of single-syllable abbreviations for the degrees of a scale: Do-Re-Me-Fa-So-La-Ti-Do.

SOPRANO
The highest-pitched general vocal range.

SORDINO
Mute.

SPACE
The gap between the lines of a staff.

SPICCATO
A technique used by string players where the bow is bounced off the strings.

STACCATO
Literally meaning "detached," staccato notes or chords are dramatically reduced in length creating a "stabbing" effect. Usually shown in notation by a dot or an arrow head above or below the note.

STAFF
A group of horizontal parallel lines and spaces on which notes are placed to define their pitch. Sometimes also called a "stave" in the singular, but always "staves" in the plural.

STEM
The vertical line attached to the head of the note. The value of the note can be progressively halved by adding a tail (or flag) to the tip of the stem.

STEP
An interval of a major 2nd or two half steps.

STRETTO
An instruction to quicken the tempo; overlapping elements in a fugue.

SUBDOMINANT
The fourth degree of a major scale.

SUBMEDIANT
The sixth degree of a major scale. Sometimes also called the superdominant.

SUPERTONIC
The second degree of the major scale.

SYMPHONY
A work for orchestra which is made up from a series of independent movements.

SYNCOPATION
A rhythm that runs against the prevailing meter or pulse, emphasizing the off-beats.

TABLATURE
A type of diagramatic notation used for fretted instruments that illustrates the positions of notes on the frets and strings. At its simplest, tablature describes just the fingering. More complex versions that incorporate note values are also possible.

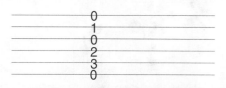

C MAJOR GUITAR CHORD
(FRET POSITIONS ON THE SIX STRINGS)

TEMPO
The speed at which the music is performed, usually measured in beats per second for a specific note type; see also Metronome.

TENEREZZA/TERAMENTE
Instruction to play tenderly.

TENOR
The vocal range directly above bass; the highest natural range for male vocalists.

TENUTO

An instruction that a note or chord should be held for at least its full duration, in some cases creating the effect of delaying the note that follows. The opposite of staccato.

TIE

A curved line joining two notes of the same pitch which indicates that the value of the second note must be added to the value of the first, and that the second note itself is NOT played. Mostly used to sustain notes across bar lines. Also known as "binds."

TIME SIGNATURE

The numerical symbols positioned at the beginning of a staff to indicate its meter. The upper number indicates the number of beats in the bar; the lower number shows the type of note that makes up those beats.

TONALITY

The relationship of notes organized within a scale to a defined tonal center. Music which can be described as tonal has an identifiable key.

TONE

British term for a step. Also a description of the color or quality of a sound.

TONIC

The first degree of a scale.

TOSTO

Instruction to play swiftly or rapidly.

TRANQUILLO

An instruction to play in calm manner.

TRANSPOSITION

A piece of music rewritten at a different pitch to the original. Usually defined in terms of the difference in interval between the two.

TREMOLO

An ornamental effect based around the fast repetition of a single note. For bowed string players this is often created by the rapid up-and-down motion of the bow; the term is also sometimes used to describe the vibrato effect used by string players created by the rapid "rolling" of the left hand.

TRIAD

A chord made up of three notes separated by intervals of a 3rd. There are four different forms (from left to right): major; minor; diminished; and augmented.

TRILL

A rapid alteration of two notes over a distance of a step or half step.

TRISTE/TRISTAMENTE

An instruction for the performer to play with a mood of sadness.

TRITONE

See diabolus in musica.

TRONCA

Cut off; accented.

TROPPO, NON
Literally meaning "not too much."

TRIPLET
A group of three notes played in the time of two.

TUNE
A melody; adjusting an instrument to concert pitch.

TURN
An ornamentation in which a marked note is played as a fast succession of notes either side of its pitch.

TUTTI
Literally meaning "all," an instruction in a score that relates to everyone, not just the soloist.

UNISON
An interval of the same pitch.

VIBRATO
A slight fluctuation in pitch, not great enough to be defined as an interval.

VIVACE
An instruction to play in a lively or brisk manner.

VOLANTE
Literally meaning "flying," an instruction to play fast.

VOLTI SUBITO (V.S.)
Instruction to turn the sheet of music quickly.

WHOLE-TONE SCALE
Six-note scale comprising major 2nd intervals. Also known as an "augmented scale."

WOLF NOTE
A note on any type of acoustic instrument that is markedly different in tone or quality to the others, resulting from the acoustic properties of the instrument.

FOREIGN EQUIVALENTS

The table below shows the note names and other musical terms in the major musical languages.

ENGLISH	FRENCH	GERMAN	ITALIAN
A	LA	A	LA
A SHARP	LA DIÉSE	AIS	LA DIESIS
A FLAT	LA BÉMOL	AES	LA BEMOLLE
B	SI	H	SI
B SHARP	SI DIÉSE	HIS	SI DIESIS
B FLAT	SI BÉMOL	B	SI BEMOLLE
C	UUT	C	DO
C SHARP	UT DIÉSE	CIS	DO DIESIS
C FLAT	UT BÉMOL	CES	DO BEMOLLE
D	RÉ	D	RE
D SHARP	RÉ DIÉSE	DIS	RE DIESIS
D FLAT	RÉ BÉMOL	D	RE BEMOLLE
E	MI	E	MI
E SHARP	MI DIÉSE	EIS	MI DIESIS
E FLAT	MI BÉMOL	EES	MI BEMOLLE
F	FA	F	FA
F SHARP	FA DIÉSE	FIS	FA DIESIS
F FLAT	FA BÉMOL	FES	FA BEMOLLE
G	SOL	G	SOL
G SHARP	SOL DIÉSE	GIS	SOL DIESIS
G FLAT	SOL BÉMOL	GES	SOL BEMOLLE
MAJOR	MAJEUR	DUR	MAGGORE
MINOR	MINEUR	MOLL	MINORE
SHARP	DIÉSE	KREUTZ	DIESIS
DOUBLE-SHARP	DOUBLE-DIÉSE	DOPPEL-KREUTZ	DOPPIO DIESIS
FLAT	BÉMOL	BE	BEMOLLE
DOUBLE FLAT	DOUBLE BÉMOL	DOPPEL-BE	DOPPIO-BEMOLLE
NATURAL	BÉCARRE	AUFLÖSUNGS-ZEICHEN	BEQUADRO
WHOLE NOTE (BRITAIN—SEMIBREVE)	RONDE	GANZE	SEMIBREVE
HALF NOTE (BRITAIN—MINIM)	BLANCHE	HALBE	BIANCA
QUARTER NOTE (BRITAIN—CROTCHET)	NOIRE	VIERTEL	NERA
EIGHTH NOTE (BRITAIN—QUAVER)	CROCHE	ACHTEL	CROMA
SIXTEENTH NOTE (BRITAIN—SEMIQUAVER)	DOUBLE-CROCHE	SECHT-ZEHNTEL	SEMI-CROMA
THIRTY-SECOND NOTE (BRITAIN—DEMI-SEMIQUAVER)	TRIPLE-CROCHE	ZWEIUND-DREISSIGSTEL	BISCROMA
SIXTY-FOURTH NOTE (BRITAIN—HEMI-DEMISEMIQUAVER)	QUADRUPLE--CROCHE	VIERUND-SECHZIGSTEL	SEMI-BISCROMA

Answers

If you follow this tutor through from the start you should eventually be tested a total of 29 times These tests of your progress and understanding are very important. If you get any of the answers wrong, go back to the relevant page in the book and ensure that you understand why it is wrong. Try to figure out how you went wrong by comparing the answer you gave with the one given here.

TEST 1 (PAGE 13)

1. A.
2. B.
3. A.
4. D.
5. B.
6. D.
7. C.
8. A.

TEST 2 (PAGE 15)

Exercise 1   C, A, G, E, F, B, E, F.
Exercise 2   C, G, B, D, D, F, A, G.
Exercise 3   F, B, A, G, C, G, C, D.
Exercise 4   F, E, D, G, B, C, D, E.
Exercise 5   G, D, G, C, G, D, C, B.

TEST 3 (PAGE 17)

Exercise 1   F, D, A, C, G, B, A, D.
Exercise 2   E, F, D, A, G, E, C, G.

TEST 4 (PAGE 20)

Exercise 1   C♯, F♯, E♭, F♯, F (F natural), E♭, G♯, F♯.
Exercise 2   B♭, F♯, D♭, C♯, G♯, F♯, B♭, B.
Exercise 3   C♯, G♯, D♭, G♯, G, B♭, C, A♯.
Exercise 4   C, B, C♯, D, B♭, E♭, F, G.
Exercise 5   F♯, C♯, G♯, C♯, E, A, G, G♯.

TEST 5 (PAGE 21)

Exercise 1   Note 3 (E)—it is F on the CD.
Exercise 2   Note 2 (D)—it repeats C on the CD.
Exercise 3   Note 4 (E)—it plays D on the CD.
Exercise 4   Note 1 (C)—it plays D on the CD.
Exercise 5   Note 4 (C)—it plays E on the CD.
Exercise 6   Note 2 (C)—it plays B on the CD.

TEST 6 (PAGE 27)

Check your answers against CD tracks 2/10, 2/11, 2/12, 2/13 and 2/14.

TEST 7 (PAGE 30)

Check your answers against CD tracks 2/18, 2/19 and 2/20.

TEST 8 (PAGE 32)

Exercise 1   Refer to CD track 2/22.
Notes: C, F, E, D, E, C, G, F, F♯, F.
Exercise 2   Refer to CD track 2/23.
Notes: C, B, A, G, C, C, D, F, D, G, F.
Exercise 3   Refer to CD track 2/24.
Notes: B, A, G, A, B, D, C, B, A.
Exercise 4   Refer to CD track 2/25.
Notes: C, G, A, F, C, A, F, C, D, F, E, G, F.
Exercise 5   Refer to CD track 2/26.
Notes: C, E, F, G, G, A, F, D, E, F, G, A, B.

TEST 9 (PAGE 33)

Staff C matches track 2/27 on the CD.

TEST 10 (PAGE 33)

As the time signature is four-four, each bar should total four beats. In fact, both bars total more than this figure because bar one has a half beat too many and bar two has two beats too many.

One solution would be simply to change the value of the quarter-note rest (one beat) in bar one to an eighth-note rest (half a beat). This would lose the surplus half beat.

In bar two, a half-note rest (two beats) could be substituted for the whole-note rest (four beats). This cuts the total back from six beats to four beats and therefore corrects the bar value.

TEST 11 (PAGE 37)

Exercise 1   Refer to CD track 3/6.
Notes: F, E, C, D, E, F, E, D, B♭, C, D, E, F.

Exercise 2   Refer to CD track 3/7.
Notes: G, A, B, C, D, B, E, F♯, G, F, E, D.
Exercise 3   Refer to CD track 3/8.
Notes: F♯, G, G♯, G, G♯, A, F♯.

TEST 12 (PAGE 39)

1. C major.
2. No—it uses B♭.
3. C.
4. Two.
5. No.
6. B.
7. Yes.
8. No, the fourth line.

9. The key is A major. The correct sequence of notes is: A, B, C♯, D, E, F♯ and G♯.
10. G♯.
11. Not necessarily, if you count downward the interval is seven half steps.
12. Four flats.
13. No, this can never happen in any key—the note positions fall on different lines when using different types of clef.
14. Yes—E.
15. No.
16. They have the same pitch but they are not technically the same note.
17. No—the key of C has no sharps.
18. Three.
19. B♭ and E♭.
20. Yes, C and B respectively. As the two keys are a half step apart, ALL of the degrees are also a half step apart.

TEST 13 (PAGE 46)

1. Four-four.
2. Four-four.
3. Three-four.
4. Three-four.
5. Six-eight.
6. Two-four.
7. Three-four.
8. Two-four.

TEST 14 (PAGE 47)

1. Time signature: Four-four.
    Key: C major.
    Notes: E, G, A, B, A, G, F, G.
2. Time signature: Four-four.
    Key: A major.
    Notes: A, B, C♯, D, E.
3. Time signature: Three-four.
    Key: D major.
    Notes: B.
4. Time signature: Five-four
    Key: C major.
    Notes: C, D, E, F, E, D, F.
5. Time signature: Twelve-eight.
    Key: F major.
    Notes: F, A, B♭, C, D, E, D, C, B♭, A.

TEST 14 (CONTINUED)

6. Time signature: Two-four.
   Key: B major.
   Notes: F#, G#, A#, B, G#.

TEST 15 (PAGE 54)

1. B, F#, G#.
2. G, C.
3. F, C#.
4. B♭, D, F#.
5. B, D, A#.
6. B♭, F, E.

TEST 16 (PAGE 55)

1. Natural minor.
2. Melodic minor.
3. Natural minor.
4. Harmonic minor.
5. Melodic minor.
6. Harmonic minor.
7. Natural minor.
8. Melodic AND Natural minor (the two scales are the same when played descending).

TEST 17 (PAGE 59)

1. C-C   (Octave).
2. D-F#   (Major 3rd).
3. B♭-E♭   (Perfect 4th).
4. E-F#   (Major 2nd).
5. A-G#   (Major 7th).
6. F-B♭   (Perfect 4th).
7. G-E   (Major 6th).
8. C-E   (Major 3rd).
9. D-B   (Major 6th).
10. B-D#   (Major 3rd).
11. A-F#   (Major 6th).
12. C-B♭   (Minor 7th).
13. F-D   (Major 6th).
14. G-D   (Perfect 5th).
15. E♭-G   (Major 3rd).
16. A-F#   (Major 6th).
17. F-E   (Major 7th).
18. C-B   (Major 7th).
19. B♭-E♭   (Perfect 4th).
20. E♭-B♭   (Perfect 5th).

21. G-A   (Major 2nd).
22. F-D   (Major 6th).
23. D-C#   (Major 7th).
24. G-F#   (Major 7th).
25. A♭-B♭   (Major 2nd).
26. D-D   (Octave).
27. A-C#   (Major 3rd).
28. G-C   (Perfect 4th).
29. B♭-D   (Major 3rd).
30. E-G#   (Major 3rd).
31. B♭-E♭   (Perfect 4th).
32. A-G#   (Augmented 5th).
33. A-G   (Minor 7th).
34. B-C   (Minor 2nd).
35. A-F   (Minor 6th).
36. B-A#   (Major 7th).
37. E-A#   (Augmented 4th).
38. A-F   (Minor 6th).
39. C-A#   (Augmented 6th).
40. F-A   (Augmented 3rd).

Note that exercises 33 to 40 are set on the bass clef.

TEST 18 (PAGE 60)

1. Perfect 5th (harmonic).
2. Major 2nd (melodic).
3. Minor 7th (harmonic).
4. Major 2nd (harmonic).
5. Perfect 4th (melodic).
6. Major 6th (melodic).
7. Minor 3rd (melodic).
8. Major 7th (harmonic).
9. Minor 3rd (harmonic).
10. Perfect 5th (melodic).

TEST 19 (PAGE 63)

1. Major 2nd.
2. Perfect 5th.
3. Minor 3rd.
4. Minor 6th.
5. Major 7th.
6. Augmented 5th.
7. Diminished 5th.
8. Diminished 2nd.
9. Minor 6th.
10. Perfect 4th.

TEST 19 (CONTINUED)

11. Perfect 5th.
12. Diminished 4th.
13. Augmented 5th.
14. Minor 3rd.
15. Major 6th.
16. Major 2nd.
17. Minor 3rd.
18. Diminished 5th.
19. Augmented 4th.
20. Diminished octave.

TEST 20 (PAGE 64)

1. C-G (Perfect 12th).
2. E-C# (Major 13th).
3. B-E♭ (Diminished 11th).
4. G-E (Major 13th).
5. B♭-F (Perfect 12th).
6. F#-D# (Major 13th).
7. A-F (Minor 13th).
8. G-D (Perfect 12th).

TEST 21 (PAGE 67)

1. Transposed to E major.

2. Transposed to A major.

3. Transposed to C major.

4. Transposed to E♭ major.

5. Transposed to D major.

6. Transposed to C major.

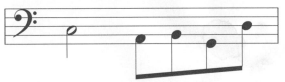

7. Transposed to A major.

8. Transposed to D♭ major.

9. Transposed to G major.

10. Transposed to A♭ major.

TEST 22 (PAGE 70)

1. G augmented.
2. D major.
3. F major.
4. A minor.
5. B♭ minor.
6. G major.
7. A diminished.
8. E augmented.

TEST 23 (PAGE 71)

1. Major.
2. Minor.
3. Diminished.
4. Minor.
5. Augmented.
6. Major.

TEST 24 (PAGE 73)

1. C major, first inversion.
2. C major, open position.
3. E minor, first inversion.
4. A minor, first inversion.
5. D major, first inversion.
6. F major, second inversion.
7. C diminished, second inversion.
8. C major, open position, second inversion.
9. C augmented, second inversion.
10. B major, second inversion.

TEST 25 (PAGE 75)

1. C major.
2. D major.
3. C major.
4. A minor.
5. E major.
6. F major.
7. D minor.

TEST 26 (PAGE 76)

1. Dominant 7th.
2. Major 7th.
3. Dominant 7th.
4. Minor 7th.
5. Half-diminished 7th.

6. Minor 7th.
7. Major 7th.
8. Half-diminished 7th.

TEST 27 (PAGE 85)

(See staves on the opposite page)

Bar 1

Replace the tied half note and quarter note with a dotted half note.

Bar 2

The three tied quarter notes are replaced by a dotted half note.

Bar 3

The beam of eight eighth notes must be broken up into a group of four and a group of two (four is the maximum that can be used in a time signature of four-four). The two tied eighth notes at the end of the beam are replaced by a single quarter note.

Bar 4

No change.

Bar 5

As the four beamed eighth notes take up the middle two beats of the bar they must be broken up into two pairs to fit in with the beat.

Bar 6

No change.

Bar 7

The tied quarter notes are replaced by a half note. The stems on the beamed eighth notes would also be better shown pointing in the opposite direction.

Bar 8

There is one beat too many in this bar. The two tied half notes could be turned into a whole note and the quarter-note rest thrown away. Alternatively, the final note could be made a dotted half note, allowing the quarter-note rest to remain in place.

Key Signature

With its six sharps, we can tell immediately that the key signature of the music is F♯—thus the scale notes are F♯, G♯, A♯, B, C♯, D♯, E♯, and F♯.

Notes

Bar 1 F♯, G♯.
Bar 2 A♯, G♯, A♯.

BAR 1 · BAR 2 · BAR 3

BAR 4 · BAR 5 · BAR 6

BAR 7 · BAR 8

TEST 27 (CONTINUED)

Bar 3 B, C♯, D♯, E♯, F♯, G♯, A♯.

Bar 4 C♯.

Bar 5 B, A♯, B, A♯, F♯.

Bar 6 G♯.

Bar 7 B, A♯, G♯, E♯.

Bar 8 F♯.

TEST 28 (PAGE 91)

1. Major.

2. Minor pentatonic.

3. Whole-tone/augmented.

4. Major pentatonic.

5. Natural minor.

6. Minor pentatonic.

7. Melodic minor.

8. Harmonic minor.

TEST 29 (PAGE 99)

To aid interpretation the sequence has been divided into repeated sections:

1. A, B, C, D (repeat from start).

2. A, B, C, D (ignore repeat), E, F (repeat from bar E).

3. E, F (ignore repeat) G (repeat from the sign).

4. B, C, D (ignore repeat), E, F (ignore repeat), G (ignore *dal segno*), H (return to *da capo*).

5. A, B, C, D (ignore repeat), E, F (ignore repeat), G (ignore *dal segno*), <u>ignore</u> bar H and play bar I to *fine*.

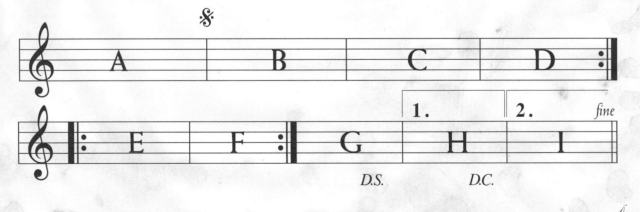

Index

Acknowlegements and Bibliography

Terence Ashley would like to thank the following people for their help with this project: Michelle Pickering at Carlton Books; Hugh Schermuly for his design expertise; Andrew O'Brien for his corrections and suggestions; Nick Kaçal for dealing with dull queries relating to music theory; and, of course, Junoir.

Derek Bailey—*Improvisation* (Moorland, 1980)
David Bowman and Paul Terry—*Aural Matters* (Schott, 1993)
Terry Burrows—*Total Guitar Tutor* (Carlton, 1998)
Terry Burrows—*Play Rock Guitar* (Dorling Kindersley, 1995)
Terry Burrows—*Play Country Guitar* (Dorling Kindersley, 1995)
Richard Chapman—*The Complete Guitarist* (Dorling Kindersley 1993)
Ralph Denyer—*The Guitar Handbook* (Pan, 1992)
Juan Martín—*El Arte De Flamenco de La Guitarra* (United Music, 1982)
Don Randall—*The New Harvard Dictionary Of Music* (Harvard University Press, 1986)

Darryl Runswick—*Rock, Jazz and Pop Arranging* (Faber and Faber, 1992)
Erik Satie—*A Mammal's Notebook: Collected Writings...* (Atlas, 1996)
Aaron Shearer—*Classic Guitar Technique* (Franco Colombo, 1963)
Nicolas Slonimsky—*Thesaurus of Scales and Melodic Patterns* (Scrivener's, 1947)
Eric Taylor—*The AB Guide to Music Theory* (Associated Board, 1989)
Jason Waldron—*Progressive Classical Guitar* (Koala, 1992)
101 Folk Songs for Buskers (Wise, 1989).